Othello

·莎翁戏剧经典·

奥瑟罗

〔英〕威廉·莎士比亚 著
申恩荣 注释

2016年·北京

威廉·莎士比亚

图 1

图 2（见 4 页）

RODERIGO

Tush, never tell me! I take it much unkindly
That thou, Iago, who hast had my purse
As if the strings were thine, shouldst know of this.

IAGO

'Sblood, but you will not hear me!
If ever I did dream of such a matter,
Abhor me.

图 3（见 10 页）

Enter Brabantio above, at a window
BRABANTIO
What is the reason of this terrible summons?
What is the matter there?

图 4(见 18 页)

IAGO   Nay, but he prated
And spoke such scurvy and provoking terms
Against your honour,
That with the little godliness I have,
I did full hard forbear him.

图 5（见 32 页）

DUKE

What in your own part can you say to this?

图 6（见 36 页）

OTHELLO
Her father loved me, oft invited me,
Still questioned me the story of my life
From year to year — the battles, sieges, fortunes
That I have passed.

图 7（见 40 页）

DESDEMONA　　　　　　　My noble father,
I do perceive here a divided duty:
To you I am bound for life and education;
My life and education both do learn me
How to respect you.

图 8（见 54 页）

IAGO
I have't. it is engendered. Hell and night
Must bring this monstrous birth to the world's light.

图 9（见 56 页）

MONTANO

Methinks the wind does speak aloud at land;
A fuller blast ne'er shook our battlements.

图 10（见 70 页）

DESDEMONA My dear Othello!
OTHELLO
It gives me wonder great as my content
To see you here before me. O, my soul's joy!

图 11（见 80 页）

CASSIO Welcome, Iago; we must to the watch.
IAGO Not his hour, Lieutenant; 'tis not yet ten o'th'-clock. Our General cast us thus early for the love of his Desdemona; who let us not therefore blame.

图 12（见 100 页）

CASSIO I have well approved it, sir. I drunk!
IAGO You or any man living may be drunk at a time, man.

图 13（见 104 页）

IAGO
How poor are they that have not patience!
What wound did ever heal but by degrees?
Thou know'st we work by wit, and not by witchcraft,
And wit depends on dilatory time.

图 14（见 106 页）

CASSIO
Masters, play here — I will content your pains —
Something that's brief; and bid 'Good morrow, General'.

图 15（见 112 页）

CASSIO Ay, but, lady,
That policy may either last so long,
Or feed upon such nice and waterish diet,
Or breed itself so out of circumstance,
That I being absent and my place supplied,
My General will forget my love and service.

图 16（见 120 页）

OTHELLO

Indeed? Ay, indeed. Discern'st thou aught in that?
Is he not honest?

IAGO Honest, my lord?

图 17（见 148—150 页）

OTHELLO
Damn her, lewd minx! O, damn here, damn her!
Come go with me apart. I will withdraw
To furnish me with some swift means of death
For the fair devil. Now art thou my Lieutenant.

图 18（见 170—172 页）

OTHELLO

Lie with her? Lie on her? We say lie on her
when they belie her. Lie with her! Zounds, that's fulsome! Handkerchief — confession — handkerchief!
To confess and be hanged for his labour.

图 19（见 174 页）

IAGO
There's many a beast then in a populous city,
And many a civil monster.

图 20（见 192—194 页）

EMILIA
For if she be not honest, chaste, and true,
There's no man happy. The purest of their wives
Is foul as slander.

图 21（见 200 页）

EMILIA He that is yours, sweet lady.
DESDEMONA
I have none. Do not talk to me, Emilia;
I cannot weep; nor answers have I none,
But what should go by water.

图 22（见 202 页）

DESDEMONA

I do not know: I am sure I am none such.

IAGO

Do not weep, do not weep. Alas the day!

图 23（见 220 页）

DESDEMONA

Good night, good night. God me such uses send,
Not to pick bad from bad, but by bad mend!

图 24（见 222 页）

IAGO
Here, at thy hand: be bold, and take thy stand.

图 25(见 224 页)

CASSIO

I am maimed for ever. Help, ho! Murder, murder!

图 26（见 236—238 页）

DESDEMONA　　　　　　　　　Ay, my lord.
OTHELLO
If you bethink yourself of any crime
Unreconciled as yet to heaven and grace,
Solicit for it straight.

图 27（见 268 页）

OTHELLO
I kissed thee, ere I killed thee: no way but his,
Killing myself, to die upon a kiss.

> *He falls on the bed and dies*

...

LODOVICO
                     O, Spartan dog,
More fell than anguish, hunger, or the sea,
Look on the tragic loading of this bed:
This is thy work.

图 28（见 268 页）

LODOVICO
The object poisons sight:
Let it be hid.

"莎翁戏剧经典"丛书总序

莎士比亚（William Shakespeare，1564—1616）是英国16世纪文艺复兴时期的伟大剧作家和诗人，也是世界文坛上的巨擘。他一生创作了38部戏剧作品（一说37部），诗作包括两部长篇叙事诗、一部十四行诗集以及其他一些短篇诗作。四百多年来这些作品被翻译成多种文字，在世界各地广泛传播。正如他同时代的批评家和剧作家本·琼生所说，他是"时代的灵魂"，"不属一个时代，而属于所有的时代！"莎士比亚在世期间，他的戏剧作品曾吸引了大量观众，包括宫廷王室成员和普通百姓，产生了巨大影响。18世纪以来，这些作品始终活跃在舞台上，20世纪随着电影业的发展，它们又被搬上银幕。几百年来，无论是体现莎士比亚原作的表演还是经过不断改编的作品，莎剧都拥有众多的观者，散发出不灭的艺术光辉；另一方面，自1623年莎士比亚全集第一对开本问世，莎士比亚的戏剧也成为学者和广大普通读者阅读、学习、研究的对象，在历代读者的阅读和研究中，这些作品不断得到新阐释和挖掘。莎士比亚的作品焕发着永久不衰的生命活力。

1564年4月，莎士比亚出生于英格兰中部的埃文河畔的斯特拉福镇。家境殷实，父亲曾经营手套和羊毛，并做过小镇的镇长。莎士比亚小时曾在镇上的文法学校读书，受到过较为正规的拉丁文和古典文学的教育。不久，家道中落，陷入经济困境，这可能成为莎士比亚后来未能进入大学读书的原因。1582年，莎士比亚十八岁时与邻村一位大他八岁的女子安·哈撒韦成婚，六个月后，大女儿苏珊娜降生，此后他们又有了一对孪生子女，不幸的是，儿子哈姆内特早夭。16世纪90年代左右，莎士比亚来到伦敦，发展他的戏剧事业。他曾是剧团的演员、编剧和股东。90年代初期，莎士比亚即开始戏剧创作。1592年，莎士比亚已在同行中崭露头角,被当时的"大学才子"剧作家格林所嫉妒,他把莎士比亚称作"那只新抖起来的乌鸦","借我们的羽毛来打扮自己……狂妄地幻想着能独自震撼(Shake-scene)这个国家的舞台"。1592—1594年间,伦敦因流行瘟疫,大部分剧院关闭,在此期间莎士比亚完成了两部著名的长篇叙事诗《维纳斯与阿多尼斯》与《鲁克丽丝受辱记》。1594年剧院恢复营业之后,莎士比亚加入宫廷大臣剧团,并终生服务于该剧团,直到1613年离开伦敦返回家乡。90年代中期,他进入了戏剧创作的巅峰时期。在1590年至1613年的二十多年之间,莎士比亚共创作了历史剧、悲剧、喜剧、传奇剧等38部。90年代中后期,他的创作以喜剧和历史剧为主,包括喜剧《仲夏夜之梦》(1595)、《威尼斯商人》(1596)、《无事生非》(1598—1599)、《皆大欢喜》(1599—1600)等和大部分历史剧,如《理查三世》(1592—1593)、《亨利四世》(上、下)(1596—1598)、《亨利五世》(1598—1599)等。这一时期,他的创作风格较为明快,充满积极向上的格调,即便剧中有悲剧的成分,整个作品也透露出对生活的肯定,对理想的向往,如《罗密欧与朱丽叶》(1595)。进入17世纪后,莎士比亚的戏剧更多地转向对人生重大问题的思考,探索解决人生之困顿的途径,诸如权力、欲望、嫉妒、暴政等等。四大悲剧《哈姆莱特》(1600—1601)、《奥瑟罗》(1603—1604)、《李尔王》(1605—1606)、《麦克白》(1606)均完成于这一时期。此外,几部重要的罗马题材剧也在90年代末和新世纪的最初几年完成,如《裘力·凯撒》(1599)、《安东尼与克里奥佩特拉》(1606)、《科里奥兰纳斯》(1608)等。莎士比亚这一时期也创作了几部喜剧,但风格较前一时期更多悲情色彩,更为沉重而引人深思。1609年,莎士比亚《十四行诗集》出版。晚期的莎士比亚剧作风格有一定变化,最有影响的是传奇剧,如《暴风雨》,通过想象的世界与现实世界的对照来探讨人生问题。

莎士比亚的名字开始传入中国是在19世纪中上叶,他的戏剧被翻译成汉语而为国人所知则是在20世纪初期。当时,他剧作的内容通过英国19世纪兰姆姐弟《莎士比亚戏剧故事集》的汉译被介绍到中国来,即无译者署名的《澥外奇谭》(1903)和林纾、魏易翻译的《吟边燕语》(1904)。20世纪20年代,莎剧汉译事业的开拓者田汉翻译了《哈孟雷特》(1921)和《罗密欧与朱丽叶》(1924)。此后,朱生豪、梁实秋、孙大雨、曹禺、曹未风、虞尔昌等译家都翻译过莎士比亚的剧作。朱生豪先生在经历日本侵略的苦难、贫穷和疾病折磨的极其艰苦的环境下,以惊人的毅力和顽强的意志,克服种种艰难险阻,穷毕生之精力完成了31部半莎剧的翻译,成为播撒莎士比亚文明之火的普罗米修斯,译莎事业的英雄和圣徒。他的莎剧译文优美畅达,人物性格鲜明,成为广大读者所珍爱的艺术瑰宝。梁实秋是中国迄今为止唯一一位个人独立完成莎剧和莎诗汉译工程的翻译家。梁译有详尽的注释和说明,学术含量较高。1956年,卞之琳翻译的《哈姆雷特》出版,他完善了孙大雨提出的翻译原则,提出"以顿代步、韵式依原诗、等行翻译"的翻译方法,可谓开一代诗体译法之风,他的译本至今都被视作该剧最优秀的译本。方平是另一位重要的成绩卓著的莎剧翻译家。2000年由他主编主译的《新莎士比亚全集》出版,其中25部莎剧由方平翻译,其他作品由阮坤、吴兴华、汪义群、覃学岚、屠岸、张冲等译出,为国内目前首部全部由分行诗体翻译的莎剧莎诗全集。

时至今日,莎士比亚的戏剧作品仍不断有新的译本出版,对广大读者而言,阅读汉译的莎剧已经是一件十分方便的事情,而这些汉译莎剧作品中不乏优秀的译本。然而,尽管莎剧的汉译丰富多彩,莎剧的改编层出不穷,要想真正了解莎剧的本来面目,我们还须要回到莎剧原文本身。其中的原因有三:一、每一种语言都是丰富的,其表达的意义可能是多元多面的,但由于译出语和译入语两种语言之间的差异,再好的翻译也只能尽可能地贴近原文而不可能百分之百地再现原文的魅力,因此,阅读再好的译本也无法取代或等同于阅读原作;二、莎士比亚生活的时代距今已经有约400年,他所使用的英语与今天人们所熟悉的英语已有较大差异,当时的人们所熟悉的文化和历史事件也是我们今天并不熟知的,因此,要真正领悟他的作品,还须回到他那时的语言和文化中去;三、莎剧经过约400年的变迁,在改编中不断变换,有些已经走出了莎士比亚时代的莎剧,因而,想要认识和了解莎剧,最佳的办法还是回到莎剧的原文本中去。

莎士比亚生活和创作的时期在16世纪末17世纪初。英语在当时已经得到极大的发展,十分活跃而成熟,尤其莎士比亚戏剧中所运用的英语,文辞丰富、结构灵活、表达力很强。但随着时代的发展,其中的一些用词、用语以及语义等都发生了变化,与我们今天的英语存在一定距离,理解起来也就会有一定困难。莎剧在绝大多数情况下采用的是诗体写作,即人物的语言是分行的,每行十个音节,轻重音节相间,一轻一重的每两个音节构成一个音步,不押韵,因此,他的剧作均为抑扬格五音步的素体诗。这样的诗体形式突显出莎剧语言的艺术魅力,音韵优美、铿锵,节奏感强,表达生动有力。然而,正因为这是诗体写作,在语法上就可能出现诗语言特有的结构,比如倒装句或词序颠倒的现象等。莎剧的语言丰富多彩,不同人物的话语呈现出多种特色,时而体现出古典拉丁语的文风,时而出现双关语、俚语、隐喻等修辞手法。典故、历史事件、政治元素、宗教、生活习俗等等都可能成为今天的读者理解莎剧原文本的障碍。因而,借助良好的注释来理解莎剧的原作就成为我们了解和认识莎剧原貌的必要手段。这次由商务印书馆隆重推出的"莎翁戏剧经典"丛书,重点选出莎士比亚的12部经典剧作,在裘克安先生主编的"莎士比亚注释"丛书的基础上进行了改编修订,并加入了精美的插图。裘先生主编的"莎士比亚注释"丛书对莎剧原文做了多方面的详尽注释,对理解原文起到有效作用,在读者中有较广泛的影响。相信这套"莎翁戏剧经典"的出版会进一步推动莎剧在广大读者中的影响力,提高人们对阅读莎剧以及经典文学作品原文的兴趣和能力,产生积极的和广泛的影响。

屠岸 章燕
2013年10月4日

"莎士比亚注释"丛书总序

莎士比亚研究在新中国有过不平坦的道路和坎坷的命运。解放后不久,大家纷纷学俄语,学英语的人数骤减。研究英国文学,要看苏联人怎么说。"文革"十年,莎士比亚同其他西方"资产阶级"作家一样被打入冷宫。改革开放以后,1978年人民文学出版社出版了在朱生豪译文基础上修订补足的《莎士比亚全集》。随之又出版了一些个别剧的不同译本,如方平译的《莎士比亚喜剧五种》(1979年)和卞之琳译的《莎士比亚悲剧四种》(1988年)。梁实秋的译本,现在大陆上也可以读到了。评介和研究莎士比亚的文章,从"文革"结束后才逐渐多起来。

但是,目前多数人学习、欣赏和研究莎士比亚,是通过中译文来进行的。精通英语而研究莎士比亚的学者不是没有,然而他们人数不多,年纪却老迈了。最近若干年,才有一些年轻人到英国或美国去学习和研究莎士比亚。

1981年我就想到有必要在中国出版我们自己注释的莎士比亚著作。谈起来,许多朋友都赞成。1984年中国莎士比亚研究会筹备和成立时,我自告奋勇,联系了一些志同道合的学者,共同开始编写莎士比亚注释本。商务印书馆大力支持出版这套丛书。到2002年底已出书26种,而且第一次印刷版已全部售完。这证明这套丛书是很受欢迎的。

要知道,莎士比亚是英语文学中最优秀的代表人物,他又是英语语言大师,学习、欣赏和研究他的原著,是译文无法替代的。商务印书馆以其远见卓识,早在1910年和1921—1935年间,就出版过几种莎士比亚剧本的注释本,以满足这方面的需求。那时的教会学校学生英文水平高,能读莎著;不但大学生能读,连有些中学生都能读。可从那时以后,整整50年中国就没印过原文的莎士比亚著作。

世界各国,莎著的注释本多得不计其数。如果唯独中国没有,实在说不过去。如果没有,对于中国知识分子欣赏和研究莎士比亚十分不利。近年来,中国人学英语的越来越多了,他们的英文水平也逐渐提高了。因此,也存在着一定的读者市场。

有了注释本,可以为明天的莎士比亚研究提供一个可靠的群众基础。而译本显然不能提供可靠的基础。

莎士比亚是16、17世纪之交的作者,他写的又是诗剧。对于现代的读者,他的英语呈现着不少的困难。不要说掌握了现代英语的中国读者,就是受过一般教育的英美人士,在初读莎士比亚原著时也面临许多障碍,需要注释的帮助。

莎士比亚的时代,英语正从受屈折变化拘束的中世纪英语,向灵活而丰富的现代英语转变。拉丁语和法语当时对英语影响很大。而莎士比亚对英语的运用又有许多革新和创造。主要的困难可以归纳为以下几个方面,也就是注释要提供帮助的方面:

(一)词汇。许多词虽然拼法和现在一样,但具有不同的早期含义,不能望文生义。另有一些词拼法和现在不一样,而含义却相同。莎士比亚独创了一些词。他特别喜欢用双关语,在他创作的早期尤其如此。而双关语是无从翻译的。这是译本无论如何也代替不了注释本的原因之一。

让我们举《哈姆莱特》剧中男主角出场后最初讲的几句话为例:

King:But now,my cousin Hamlet,and my son —
Hamlet〔Aside〕:A little more than kin,and less than kind!
King:How is it that the clouds still hang on you?
Hamlet:Not so,my lord. I am too much i' the sun.

- 梁实秋的译文如下:

王:现在,我的侄儿哈姆雷特,也是我的儿子,——
哈[旁白]:比侄子是亲些,可是还算不得儿子。
王:怎么,你脸上还是罩着一层愁云?
哈:不是的,陛下;我受的阳光太多了。

- 卞之琳的译文如下:

王：得，哈姆雷特，我的侄子，我的儿——
哈〔旁白〕：亲上加亲，越亲越不相亲！
王：你怎么还是让愁云惨雾罩着你？
哈：陛下，太阳大，受不了这个热劲"儿"。

- 朱生豪的译文如下：

王：可是来，我的侄儿哈姆莱特，我的孩子——
哈〔旁白〕：超乎寻常的亲族，漠不相干的路人。
王：为什么愁云依旧笼罩在你的身上？
哈：不，陛下；我已经在太阳里晒得太久了。

这里，主要困难在于莎士比亚让哈姆莱特使用了 kin 和 kind 以及 son 和 sun 两组双关语。kind 一词又有双关意义，翻译无法完全表达，只能各译一个侧面。结果，梁和卞两先生还得用注释补足其义，朱译则连注释也没有。这种地方，能读原文注释本的人才能充分领略莎氏原意。

哈姆莱特在旁白里说：比亲戚多一点——本来我是你的侄子，现在又成了你的儿子，确实不是一般的亲戚关系啊；然而却比 kind 少一点——kind 有两层意思，一是"同类相求"的亲近感，一是"与人为善"的善意感，我同你没有共同语言，我也不知道你是安的什么心。这话只能对自己说，在舞台上假定对方是听不到的。哈姆莱特的第二句话是公开的俏皮话：哪里有什么阴云呀，我在太阳里晒得不行呢。sun 是跟 clouds 相对；太阳又意味着国王的恩宠，"你对我太好了，我怎么会阴郁呢？"sun 又跟 son 谐音，"做你的儿子，我领教得够了。"原文并不是像梁实秋所说的那样晦涩难解。可是含义太复杂，有隐藏的深层感情，所以无法译得完全。

（二）语法。有些现象，按现代英语语法的标准看，似乎是错误的，但在当时并不错，是属于中世纪英语的残余因素。例如有些动词过去分词的词尾变化、代词的所有格形式、主谓语数的不一致、关系代词和介词的用法等方面，都有一些和现在不同的情况。注释里说明了，可以举一反三去理解。

（三）词序的颠倒和穿插。词尾屈折变化较多的中世纪英语本来对词序没有严格的要求。伊丽莎白时代继承了这种习惯。同时,诗的节律和押韵要求对词序做一定的灵活处理。莎士比亚的舞台语言以鲜明、有力、生动为首要考虑,有时他就把语法和句法放在从属的地位。在激动的台词中,由于思路、感情的变化,语言也常有脱出常规的变化。这些地方,有了注释的指点,理解就容易得多。

(四)典故。莎士比亚用典很多。古希腊、罗马神话、《圣经》故事,英国民间传说,历史逸事……他都随手拈来。其中有一大部分对于英美读者来说乃是常识,但中国读者就很需要注释的帮助。

(五)文化背景。注释可以提供关于基督教义、中世纪传统观点、文艺复兴时期新的主张、英国习俗等方面的知识。

除上述以外,还有莎剧中影射时事,以及版本考据诸问题,在注释本中可以详细论述,也可以简单提及。

世界文豪莫不是语言大师,而要真正理解和欣赏一位大师的文笔,当然非读他的原著不成。出版莎士比亚注释本,首先是为了让中国读者便于买到和读到他的原著。不过我们自知现出的几十种在版本、注释和其他方面还存在不足之处,希望读者多提意见,以便今后不断改进。

裘克安

前　言

威廉·莎士比亚(William Shakespeare)出生于1564年4月。他父亲名叫约翰(John)，是英国中部埃文河畔斯特拉福镇(Stratford-on-Avon)上一个相当富裕的羊皮手套手工业者和经营羊毛皮革和谷物等的商人。1565年他担任镇政府的民政官，后来又当上了镇议员和镇长。威廉很可能在镇上一所文法学校(The Grammar School of Stratford)学习，主要读拉丁文，可能读点希腊文、哲学、修辞学、文学和历史等。1578年威廉14岁时，他父亲似乎破了产，他不得不辍学在家，帮助父亲做各种手艺和生意，据说他还当过乡间学校的助理教师。大约在1585年，威廉到了伦敦，那时他22岁。传说他曾在剧院门前为贵族顾客看马，后来在剧院里干些贱活，逐渐成为剧院的演员和股东，并开始了戏剧创作活动，起初改编别人的老剧本，然后转到独立创作。现在保存下来的37个剧本，可能不过是他在伦敦时期所写的剧本的一部分。威廉开始是向大学才子剧作家们学习，逐渐青出于蓝，卓有成就，引起他们的嫉妒。1592年，罗伯特·格林(Robert Greene)曾以讽刺的口吻影射说，他是"用我们的羽毛美化了的暴发户乌鸦。"威廉在戏剧方面获得了巨大的成功，这决不是偶然的。他在伦敦广泛接触到各阶层的人，熟悉了他们的语言，加深了对当时英国社会生活的了解；经过长时间的舞台生活，他又学会许多门径，摸熟观众的心理与兴趣所在。他的大部分剧本是利用现成材料加以改编而写成的，在改编过程中注入了新的内容和艺术加工，剧本充满着人文主义精神和迷人的魔力，他便成为极受社会欢迎的演员和剧作家而驰誉伦敦。大约在1612年，他退出舞台生涯，回到他的家乡斯特拉福镇。1616年4月23日，这位扬名千古的最杰出的诗人剧作家悄然逝世，享年52岁。

《奥瑟罗》是莎士比亚四大悲剧之一,也是他晚年成熟的诗剧名篇,是世界文学宝库中不朽之作。这部5幕15场悲剧大约写于1602年,是紧跟《哈姆莱特》之后的作品。1604年曾在詹姆斯一世王宫里演出过。

这部著名悲剧的剧情取材于意大利人吉拉尔第·秦齐奥(Giraldi Cinzio)的《故事百篇》(*Ecatommiti*),该书于1565年在威尼斯出版。剧情如下:

在威尼斯住着一个名叫奥瑟罗的摩尔人(非洲北部的黑人),他原是王室子弟,是一位人品见识都出众、精通战术的职业军人。人们称他是"高尚的、有能力的摩尔人"。但是他过分纯朴善良,相信别人,疑心逐步加深,分不出好人与坏人。他经常说,"老实人伊阿古","非常老实的伊阿古。"那时威尼斯上流社会有一位年轻貌美的苔丝狄蒙娜小姐,她活泼、温柔、思想开放,在爱情上颇有主见,她认为奥瑟罗跟其他贵族富商的纨袴子弟不一样,拒绝了众多的求婚者,偏偏爱上了奥瑟罗,并且不顾她元老父亲的反对,和他秘密结了婚。可是奥瑟罗半生戎马生涯,习惯于军营和战争生活,对于女人,特别是白种女人缺乏了解,他们就是在许多方面互相不了解的情况下结为伉俪的。

伊阿古是奥瑟罗的旗官,他对于凯西奥当上了奥瑟罗的副将怀恨在心,他是个利欲熏心,又有复仇心理的阴谋家。他首先向奥瑟罗暗示他是个黑人,而凯西奥和苔丝狄蒙娜都是威尼斯人,他们同种同性,有暧昧关系。为了证实他的谎言,他一再要他妻子爱米利娅去偷她主妇苔丝狄蒙娜的花手帕,那是奥瑟罗送给苔丝狄蒙娜的定情信物。恰巧有一次她不小心丢失了这个手帕,爱米利娅顺手捡了起来,为了满足她丈夫的好奇心,把它送给了他。伊阿古把手帕故意放到凯西奥的房间里。他回头向奥瑟罗撒谎说,"苔丝狄蒙娜把手帕送给她的情人凯西奥。"伊阿古进一步用偷梁换柱、以假乱真的手法,来毒害奥瑟罗的心灵,加深他的疑惧和嫉妒。凯西奥有个情妇比恩卡,缠着他要和他亲近。伊阿古故意唆使凯西奥谈谈他跟比恩卡的私情,并安排奥瑟罗来偷听,他就误以为凯西奥谈的是苔丝狄蒙娜。就这样奥瑟罗任凭阴谋家伊阿古的摆布，一步步跌入伊阿古设下的陷阱，他认为苔丝狄蒙娜跟妓女一样，欺骗了他，让他戴上绿帽子，头上生了两只角。他妒火中烧，疾恶如仇，一方面派伊阿古去暗杀凯西奥，结果砍断凯西奥一条腿。另一方面他不顾苔丝狄蒙娜连声喊冤叫屈，矢口否认跟凯西奥有什么私情，苦苦哀求，在盛怒和失去理性的情况下把他的爱妻活活卡死。

骇人听闻的苔丝狄蒙娜之死发生后，引起人们广泛的悲伤，爱米利娅等人纷纷起来揭发伊阿古的谎言和诡计，奥瑟罗这才猛醒过来，尝到了上坏人当的痛苦，他拔剑砍伤伊阿古的双腿，看他是否有着魔鬼一样分趾的脚，然后饮恨自杀。毒蛇般的伊阿古也得到了应有的最严厉的惩罚。

《奥瑟罗》有几个突出的特点。首先，莎士比亚以前的文学中，都把摩尔人描绘成半人半鬼的形象，莎士比亚自己在1591年写《泰特斯·安德洛尼克斯》一剧时，也把摩尔人艾伦写成连灵魂都是黑的阴谋家。而12年后，他对摩尔人的看法发生了多么大的变化！莎士比亚是第一人，排除种族偏见把奥瑟罗写成高尚的英雄人物。这是文艺复兴时代平等看待人的新观点。其次，在莎士比亚所有剧作中，《奥瑟罗》是唯一的以当代文艺复兴时代为背景的家庭剧(domestic drama)，它虽发生在威尼斯和塞浦路斯，却并非历史剧。它描写的黑白异族之间的婚姻关系有强烈的现实感。奥瑟罗带有黑人那种感情冲动，易于热血上涌趋于癫狂和相信巫术的特征，而苔丝狄蒙娜则具有意大利人的热情，她天真无邪，全身心地委托于丈夫，两人间的隔膜和过于理想化的新式恋爱关系给坏人造成可乘之机。第三，伊阿古这一角色，脱胎于中世纪道德剧中"邪恶"的典型形象。但莎士比亚将他写成有血有肉、有多种动机的活的人物，已脱离过去剧中程式化的僵死结构，随着他自己设置的诡计的发展而越走越远。

莎士比亚通过对这个有迷惑力的人物的天才刻画，显示了邪恶的巨大破坏力量，使一桩美满婚姻走向毁灭，同时也毁灭了他自己。

莎士比亚这个剧本充满了诗意的语言，他出色地使用了各种修辞手段，如譬喻、反论、意象（metaphor, paradox, imagery）。例如，他利用戏剧反讽（dramatic irony）描绘出伊阿古这个恶人多么阴险可怕，受他欺骗的人个个赞扬他老实、善良和可以信赖，心甘情愿充当他的工具，这可以说是一个精心构思出来的戏剧反讽。

《奥瑟罗》这个剧本最早分别出版于1622年的四开本和1623年的对开本，两者有些差别，但差别不是很大。一般用这两种版本相互对勘和补充而成现用的版本。为了帮助读者阅读和欣赏这一文学名著，按行码的顺序作了比较详尽的注释。除释义外，对某些语法修辞特点也作了说明。注释承裘克安先生仔细审阅并作了一些修改，特此表示衷心的感谢。

申恩荣
1993年1月于湖南师范大学外语系

OTHELLO

DRAMATIS PERSONAE

OTHELLO, a Moor, General in the Venetian army
DESDEMONA, his wife
CASSIO, his Lieutenant
IAGO, his Ancient
EMILIA, wife of Iago
BIANCA, mistress of Cassio
RODERIGO, in love with Desdemona

THE DUKE OF VENICE
BRABANTIO, a Venetian Senator, Desdemona's father
GRATIANO, his brother
LODOVICO, his kinsman
MONTANO, Governor of Cyprus

Senators of Venice
Gentlemen of Cyprus
Musicians
Officers
A Clown in Othello's household
A Herald
A Sailor
A Messenger
Soldiers, attendants, and servants

注　释

Othello [əuˈθeləu]　奥瑟罗，威尼斯将军，摩尔人。摩尔人为非洲西北部阿拉伯和柏柏尔(Berber)混血的民族，伊丽莎白时代英国人常将他们和黑人相混同。

Desdemona [dezdiˈməunə]　苔丝狄蒙娜，奥瑟罗之妻，意大利白人。

Cassio [ˈkæsiəu]　凯西奥，奥瑟罗的副将

Iago [iˈɑːgəu]　伊阿古，奥瑟罗的旗官

Emilia [iˈmiliə]　爱米利娅，伊阿古之妻

Bianca [biˈæŋkə]　比恩卡，凯西奥的情妇

Roderigo [ˌrɔdəˈrigəu]　罗德利哥，苔丝狄蒙娜的追求者

The Duke of Venice　威尼斯公爵，当时威尼斯为独立的城邦

Brabantio [brəˈbænʃiəu]　勃拉班修，威尼斯元老院议员，苔丝狄蒙娜之父

Gratiano [grɑːʃiˈɑːnəu]　葛莱西安诺，勃拉班修之弟

Lodovico [lədəuˈviːkəu]　罗多维科，勃拉班修的亲戚

Montano　蒙太诺，塞浦路斯总督，当时塞浦路斯为威尼斯的属地。

Senators of Venice　威尼斯元老院议员

ACT I

SCENE I

Venice. A Street.

I. i   *Enter Roderigo and Iago*

RODERIGO

    Tush, never tell me! I take it much unkindly
    That thou, Iago, who hast had my purse
    As if the strings were thine, shouldst know of this.

IAGO

    'Sblood, but you will not hear me!
5   If ever I did dream of such a matter,
    Abhor me.

RODERIGO

    Thou told'st me thou didst hold him in thy hate.

IAGO

    Despise me, if I do not. Three great ones of the city,
    In personal suit to make me his Lieutenant,
10 Off-capped to him: and by the faith of man,
    I know my price, I am worth no worse a place.
    But he, as loving his own pride and purposes,
    Evades them with a bombast circumstance
    Horribly stuffed with epithets of war,
15 And in conclusion
    Non-suits my mediators. For 'Certes,' says he,
    'I have already chose my officer.'
    And what was he?
    Forsooth, a great arithmetician,
20 One Michael Cassio, a Florentine —
    A fellow almost damned in a fair wife —

ACT I SCENE I

I. i（第一幕第一场，后类推）（以下黑体数字为行码）

1 Tush：啐（表示反对和鄙弃的拟声感叹词）。 **take it unkindly**：endure something with resentment.

2 had：had the use of,支配,使用。 **thou**：旧式第二人称单数代词,其动词多用结尾-st 的形式。

3 strings：purse-strings,当时钱袋用细绳收口。 **know of**：预闻。 **this**：指苔丝狄蒙娜私奔到奥瑟罗之事。因罗德利哥一直在追求苔,伊是知道的。1—3 句核心为 I resent that you should know of this. 罗怀疑伊背着他搞鬼。

4 'Sblood：(I swear by) His blood 指以耶稣流的血起誓（赌咒语）。

6 Abhor：regard with disgust.

7 hate：hatred. **him**：指奥瑟罗。 **thy**：your(thou 的所有格)。 hold sb. in one's hatred=hate sb.

9 In personal suit：in a personal request,亲自请求。

10 Off-capped to：took off their caps to,脱帽致敬。 **by the faith of man**：凭人的信仰（对上帝）起誓。

12 as：inasmuch as.

13 them：指上 three great ones. **bombast**：inflated,wordy,原意为用棉絮填充的。 **circumstance**：evasion,原意为 standing（going）around.

14 stuffed … war：padded out with military terms,充满军事用语。

16 Non-suits：rejects the suit,拒绝请求。 **mediators**：中间人,说情者。 **Certes**：truly,确实。

17 chose：chosen.

19 Forsooth：indeed,实在（带有讽刺意味）。 **arithmetician**：算术家（只会搞理论,不能务实的人）。

20 Florentine：man of Florence,佛罗伦萨人。

21 damned … wife：i. e., a sneering suggestion that Cassio's fond wish to marry a beautiful woman will be his downfall,以嘲弄的口气暗示凯西奥因为想要娶漂亮女人为妻,而几乎会毁了自己的一切。

That never set a squadron in the field,
Nor the division of a battle knows
More than a spinster — unless the bookish theoric,
Wherein the togèd consuls can propose
As masterly as he. Mere prattle without practice
Is all his soldiership. But he, sir, had th'election;
And I, of whom his eyes had seen the proof
At Rhodes, at Cyprus, and on other grounds
Christian and heathen, must be belee'd and calmed
By debitor and creditor; this counter-caster,
He in good time must his Lieutenant be,
And I — God bless the mark! — his Moorship's Ancient.

RODERIGO

By heaven, I rather would have been his hangman.

IAGO

Why, there's no remedy. 'Tis the curse of service;
Preferment goes by letter and affection,
And not by old gradation, where each second
Stood heir to th'first. Now sir, be judge yourself
Whether I in any just term am affined
To love the Moor.

RODERIGO

I would not follow him then.

IAGO   O, sir, content you;
I follow him to serve my turn upon him.
We cannot all be masters, nor all masters
Cannot be truly followed. You shall mark
Many a duteous and knee-crooking knave
That, doting on his own obsequious bondage,
Wears out his time, much like his master's ass,
For naught but provender, and when he's old — cashiered!
Whip me such honest knaves. Others there are
Who, trimmed in forms and visages of duty,

23　knows: i. e., 倒装（正常词序应在 nor 之后）。　**division**: orderly arrangement.　**battle**: battalion, armed force.

24　spinster: unmarried woman.　**unless**: but only.　**theoric**: theory.

25　togèd consuls: officials wearing togas, 身穿宽袍的参议员。**propose**: discourse, 谈论。

26　masterly: master-like, masterful.

27　election: choice for an office. the 省去 e 和 election 连读, 为了诗律中省一个音节。

28　his: i. e., Othello's.

29　Rhodes [rəudz]: 罗得岛（现属希腊）。　**Cyprus** ['saiprəs]: 地中海岛塞浦路斯, 现为独立国。

30　belee'd and calmed: left to leeward without wind and becalmed. 系航海用语, 帆船因无风停止不前（喻赋闲）。

31　debitor and creditor: 借方和贷方, 算账者（对 Cassio 的蔑指）。**counter-caster**: 用 counters 筹码, 算账的人, 同上。

33　God bless the mark!: 原意上帝祝福靶心, 为射箭时咒语。现在用为说人坏话时的插话, 意为"不客气地说", "不要怪我这样说"。**Moorship**: 仿 worship（阁下）戏撰的致敬语。　**Ancient**: ensign, 扛旗的旗官。

34　By heaven: （指天为誓）天哪。

36　letter and affection: 推荐信和偏爱。

37　gradation: 论资排辈。

38　stood: would certainly have stood.

39　term: way, respect.　**affined**: bound, compelled by duty.

41　content you: be calm.

42　serve my turn upon him: 在他身上获得我自己的目的。

43—44　nor …/Cannot: 双重否定, 这是伊丽莎白时代惯常的否定用法。　**shall**: will.　**mark**: notice.

45　knee-crooking: knee-bending, 喻 obsequious.　**knave**: servant.

48　naught but: nothing except.　**provender**: fodder, 草料。**cashiered**: dismissed with disgrace, 开除。

49　me: for me, 语法上叫 ethical dative.

50　trimmed … duty: furnished with appearances of loyalty, 表面上装出忠诚的样子。

Keep yet their hearts attending on themselves,
And, throwing but shows of service on their lords,
Do well thrive by them; and when they have lined their coats,
Do themselves homage: these fellows have some soul,
55 And such a one do I profess myself.
For, sir,
It is as sure as you are Roderigo,
Were I the Moor, I would not be Iago:
In following him, I follow but myself.
60 Heaven is my judge, not I for love and duty,
But seeming so for my peculiar end:
For when my outward action doth demonstrate
The native act and figure of my heart
In compliment extern, 'tis not long after,
65 But I will wear my heart upon my sleeve
For daws to peck at — I am not what I am.

RODERIGO

What a full fortune does the thick-lips owe
If he can carry's thus!

IAGO   Call up her father,
Rouse him, make after him, poison his delight,
70 Proclaim him in the streets; incense her kinsmen,
And, though he in a fertile climate dwell,
Plague him with flies: though that his joy be joy,
Yet throw such chances of vexation on't,
As it may lose some colour.

RODERIGO

75 Here is her father's house; I'll call aloud.

IAGO

Do, with like timorous accent and dire yell,
As when, by night and negligence, the fire
Is spied in populous cities.

RODERIGO

53 lined:原意为衬硬里,特意填充,装满钱。

54 soul:spirit.

59 but:only.

60 not I:I am not.

61 peculiar:personal.

63 native:natural, innate. **act**:action, operation. **figure**:shape, intent.

64 compliment extern:external complement (appearance, demeanour).

65 wear my heart upon my sleeve:i. e., 此为莎士比亚创造的名言。中世纪骑士惯在袖口上佩戴心爱的人的花朵,此言佩戴自己的心,意为表露自己的真心。

66 daws:jackdaws,乌鸦(喻普通的傻瓜)。 **I … am**:我是不露真心的。

67 full:perfect, very good. **thick-lips**:Negro,伊丽莎白时代英国人将其和 Moor 混同,此处指 Othello,用为单数。 **owe**:own, possess, have.

68 carry't thus:carry it (this marriage) off.

69 make after:follow, pursue.

70 Proclaim:宣扬。

71 dwell:he 的谓语,假设语气。 **fertile**:promoting fertility.

72 though that:though.

73 chances:occurrences. **on't**:on it (his joy).

74 As:so that.

76 like:likely, seemingly. **timorous accent**:frightened voice.

What, ho, Brabantio! Signor Brabantio, ho!
IAGO

Awake! What, ho, Brabantio! Thieves, thieves!
Look to your house, your daughter, and your bags!
Thieves, thieves!

Enter Brabantio above, at a window

BRABANTIO

What is the reason of this terrible summons?
What is the matter there?

RODERIGO

Signor, is all your family within?

IAGO

Are your doors locked?

BRABANTIO   Why, wherefore ask you this?

IAGO

Zounds, sir, you're robbed; for shame, put on your gown;
Your heart is burst, you have lost half your soul.
Even now, now, very now, an old black ram
Is tupping your white ewe. Arise, arise,
Awake the snorting citizens with the bell,
Or else the devil will make a grandsire of you.
Arise, I say!

BRABANTIO   What, have you lost your wits?

RODERIGO

Most reverend signor, do you know my voice?

BRABANTIO

Not I; what are you?

RODERIGO   My name is Roderigo.

BRABANTIO

The worser welcome!
I have charged thee not to haunt about my doors.
In honest plainness thou hast heard me say
My daughter is not for thee. And now in madness,
Being full of supper and distempering draughts,

79 Signor [ˈsiːnjɔː]：〈意大利语〉先生。

83 summons：call to appear.

87 'Zounds：by His wounds，凭耶稣在十字架上受的创伤起誓，诅咒语。

89—90 black … ewe：伊阿古粗野地描述这次婚姻是公羊和母羊的交配，而且暗示奥瑟罗是一个魔鬼。

90 tupping：copulating.

91 snorting：snoring.

93 wits：faculties of thinking, senses.

96 The worser welcome!：更不欢迎！

100 distempering：intemperate，过量的。 **draughts**：drinks.

Upon malicious bravery dost thou come
To start my quiet.

RODERIGO

Sir, sir, sir —

BRABANTIO But thou must needs be sure
My spirit and my place have in them power
To make this bitter to thee.

RODERIGO　　　　　　　　　　Patience, good sir.

BRABANTIO

What tell'st thou me of robbing? This is Venice;
My house is not a grange.

RODERIGO　　　　　　　　　Most grave Brabantio,
In simple and pure soul I come to you…

IAGO Zounds, sir, you are one of those that will not serve God if the devil bid you. Because we come to do you service, and you think we are ruffians, you'll have your daughter covered with a Barbary horse; you'll have your nephews neigh to you, you'll have coursers for cousins, and jennets for germans.

BRABANTIO What profane wretch art thou?

IAGO I am one, sir, that comes to tell you, your daughter and the Moor are now making the beast with two backs.

BRABANTIO

Thou art a villain.

IAGO　　　　　　　You are a Senator.

BRABANTIO

This thou shalt answer. I know thee, Roderigo.

RODERIGO

Sir, I will answer anything. But I beseech you
If't be your pleasure and most wise consent,
As partly I find it is, that your fair daughter,
At this odd-even and dull watch o'th'night,
Transported with no worse nor better guard

101　bravery：bravado.

102　start：startle，upset，扰乱。

107　grange：farmhouse.　　**grave**：worthy.

108　simple：sincere.

112　covered：copulated.　　**Barbary**：北非柏柏尔人（摩尔人）居住的地区。

113　nephews：grandsons.　　**coursers**：horses.

114　cousins：relatives.　　**jennets**：小马。　　**germants**：relatives.　　**for**：as.

117—118　beast with two backs：有两个背的兽，男女在交配状。

120　answer：pay for，atone for，account for.

124　odd-even：奇数偶数之间，确切意思不明，一般猜想意谓半夜。　**dull**：sleepy，heavy.　　**watch o'th'night**：a period of the night.

125　with：by.

But with a knave of common hire, a gondolier,
To the gross clasps of a lascivious Moor —
If this be known to you, and your allowance,
We then have done you bold and saucy wrongs;
130 But if you know not this, my manners tell me
We have your wrong rebuke. Do not believe
That from the sense of all civility
I thus would play and trifle with your reverence.
Your daughter, if you have not given her leave,
135 I say again hath made a gross revolt,
Tying her duty, beauty, wit, and fortunes
In an extravagant and wheeling stranger
Of here and everywhere. Straight satisfy yourself:
If she be in her chamber or your house,
140 Let loose on me the justice of the state
For thus deluding you.

BRABANTIO   Strike on the tinder, ho!
Give me a taper; call up all my people!
This accident is not unlike my dream:
Belief of it oppresses me already.
Light, I say, light!   *Exit above*

145 IAGO   Farewell, for I must leave you.
It seems not meet, nor wholesome to my place,
To be produced — as if I stay, I shall —
Against the Moor. For I do know the state,
However this may gall him with some check,
150 Cannot with safety cast him; for he's embarked
With such loud reason to the Cyprus wars,
Which even now stand in act, that for their souls
Another of his fathom they have none
To lead their business. In which regard,
155 Though I do hate him as I do hell pains,
Yet for necessity of present life
I must show out a flag and sign of love,

ACT I SCENE I

126　But with: than by.　**knave**: low person.　**gondolier**: 威尼斯狭长平底两头翘的船(gondola)的船夫。

127　clasps: embraces.　**lascivious**: 好色的,淫乱的。

128　and: 后省略 have.　**allowance**: permission.

129　saucy: impertinent, rude, 无礼的。　**wrongs**: 当时抽象名词可用复数。

130　manners: morals; moral character.

132　from: away from, contrary to.

133　your reverence: the respect due to you.

134　leave: permission.

135　gross: flagrant.

136　wit: intelligence.

137　extravagant: wandering beyond bonds, vagrant, 流浪的。 **wheeling**: roving.　**stranger**: foreigner 指 Othello.

138　Straight: straight way, at once.　**satisfy yourself**: convince yourself, provide yourself with adequate proof.

140　justice: law.

141　Strike … tinder: 击燧石点燃火绒(旧时取火方法)。

142　taper: 细蜡烛。

143　accident: occurrence, 事件。

146　meet: fitting, appropriate.　**wholesome**: suitable.　**place**: position, i. e., as Othello's ancient.

147　produced: brought forward.　**as**: since.

148　know: 后省略 that.　**the state**: 指威尼斯城邦。

149　gall: hurt.　**check**: reprimand, censure. 此行为插入语,主句为 the state cannot cast him.

150　cast: dismiss.　**with safety**: 插入语。　**embarked**: engaged.

151　loud: urgent.

152　stand in act: are going on.　**that**: and that.　**for their souls**: 就是交出他们的灵魂,他们也得不到…,此处 for 相当于 in exchange for.

153　fathom: grasp of intellect.

154　business: undertaking(此处指战争)。　**regard**: respect, 方面。

155　hell pains: tortures in hell.

>   Which is indeed but sign. That you shall surely find him,
>   Lead to the Sagittary the raisèd search;
> 160   And there will I be with him. So farewell. *Exit*
>   *Enter Brabantio in his night-gown with servants and
>   torches*
>
> BRABANTIO
>   It is too true an evil. Gone she is,
>   And what's to come of my despisèd time
>   Is naught but bitterness. Now, Roderigo,
>   Where didst thou see her? —O unhappy girl! —
> 165   With the Moor, say'st thou? — Who would be a father? —
>   How didst thou know 'twas she? — O, she deceives me
>   Past thought! — What said she to you? — Get more tapers.
>   Raise all my kindred. —Are they married, think you?
> RODERIGO
>   Truly I think they are.
> BRABANTIO
> 170   O heaven! How got she out? O treason of the blood!
>   Fathers, from hence trust not your daughters' minds
>   By what you see them act. Is there not charms
>   By which the property of youth and maidhood
>   May be abused? Have your not read, Roderigo,
>   Of some such thing?
> 175 RODERIGO   Yse, sir, I have indeed.
> BRABANTIO
>   Call up my brother — O would you had had her!
>   Some one way, some another. Do you know
>   Where we may apprehend her and the Moor?
> RODERIGO
>   I think I can discover him, if you please
> 180   To get good guard and go along with me.

158 That：in order that.

159 Sagittary："马人旅馆"以一个 centaur，即希腊神话中半人半马的怪物为招牌的旅店。　**raisèd search**：召集起来的搜查队。

162 my despisèd time：the rest of my despicable life.

167 Past thought：想象不到地。

168 Raise：rouse up.

170 treason ... blood：treachery of my own child.

172 charms：magic spells，魔术，咒语。谓语倒置于复数主语前时，常用单数，这里用 Is.

173 property：nature.　**maidhood**：maidenhood，少女的贞操。

174 abused：deceived.

176 O ... her!：但愿当初你娶了她！（you 指 Roderigo）

177 Some：后省略 go.

178 apprehend：捉拿。

179 discover：uncover.

180 guard：警吏。　**go**：come.

OTHELLO

BRABANTIO
    Pray you, lead on. At every house I'll call —
    I may command at most. Get weapons, ho!
    And raise some special officers of night.
    On, good Roderigo, I'll deserve your pains. *Exeunt*

SCENE II

I. ii   *Enter Othello, Iago, attendants with torches*

IAGO
    Though in the trade of war I have slain men,
    Yet do I hold it very stuff o'th'conscience
    To do no contrived murder: I lack iniquity
    Sometimes to do me service. Nine or ten times
5   I had though t'have yerked him here under the ribs.
OTHELLO
    'Tis better as it is.
IAGO   Nay, but he prated
    And spoke such scurvy and provoking terms
    Against your honour,
    That with the little godliness I have,
10 I did full hard forbear him. But I pray, sir,
    Are you fast married? For be assured of this,
    That the Magnifico is much beloved,
    And hath in his effect a voice potential
    As double as the Duke's. He will divorce you,
15 Or put upon you what restraint and grievance
    That law, with all his might to enforce it on,
    Will give him cable.
OTHELLO   Let him do his spite:
    My services, which I have done the signory,
    Shall out-tongue his complaints. 'Tis yet to know —
20 Which, when I know that boasting is an honour,
    I shall provulgate — I fetch my life and being

182　command at most：demand the assistance of the greatest number of people.

183　officers of night：巡夜的警吏。

184　On：前面省略 go.　　**deserve … pains**：reward your labour, 报答你的辛劳。

I. ii

2　very stuff：the essential substance, 本质。

3　coutrived：预谋的。　　**iniquity**：坏心眼。

5　yerked：stabbed.　　**him**：指 Roderigo.

6　prated：prattled, 胡说。

7　scurvy：下流的, 卑鄙的。　　**provoking terms**：使人恼火的言语。

10　did … him：费了很大劲才控制自己不杀他。　　**full**：very.

11　fast：securely, 稳固地。

12　the Magnifico：威尼斯贵人（指 Brabantio）.

13　in his effect：at his command.　　**potential**：powerful.

14　As double as：twice as 形容 potential.

15　grievance：oppression, annoyance.

16　might：power.

17　cable：缆绳（转义 scope, 活动余地）。　　**do … spite**：发泄他的愤恨。

18　signory：威尼斯政府。

19　out-tongue：speak louder than.　　**yet to know**：not yet generally known.

20　关系代词 which 的先行词为主句中的主语 it, 在从句中作 provulgate 的宾语。when 从句为插入语。

21　provulgate：promulgate; publish, 宣告。　　**fetch … being**：am descended.　　**life and being**：生命（此类用一对同义词构成的短语很多，如 end and aim, hustle and bustle 等）。

From men of royal siege, and my demerits
May speak, unbonneted, to as proud a fortune
As this that I have reached. For know, Iago,
But that I love the gentle Desdemona,
I would not my unhousèd free condition
Put into circumscription and confine
For the seas' worth. But look, what lights come yond!
IAGO
  Those are the raisèd father and his friends:
  You were best go in.
OTHELLO   Not I; I must be found.
  My parts, my title, and my perfect soul
  Shall manifest me rightly. Is it they?
IAGO
  By Janus, I think no.
      Enter Cassio, with men bearing torches
OTHELLO
  The servants of the Duke and my Lieutenant!
  The goodness of the night upon you, friends.
  What is the news?
CASSIO   The Duke does greet you, General,
  And he requires your haste-post-haste appearance
  Even on the instant.
OTHELLO   What is the matter, think you?
CASSIO
  Something from Cyprus, as I may divine:
  It is a business of some heat. The galleys
  Have sent a dozen sequent messengers
  This very night at one another's heels;
  And many of the consuls, raised and met,
  Are at the Duke's already. You have been hotly call for,
  When being not at your lodging to be found.
  The senate hath sent about three several quests
  To search you out.

22 **siege**:seat,rank.　**demerits**:deserts,merits,品德,功劳。

23 **speak … to**:平等交谈,配得。　**unbonneted**:不戴帽,不必另加荣誉。bonnet是威尼斯贵族戴的天鹅绒软帽。　**proud**:exalted.

25 **But that**:except that,若不是因为。

26 **unhousèd**:unrestrained,没结婚的。

27 **circumscription and confine**:羁绊,约束。

28 **For**:in exchange for.　**the seas'**:海洋中有所有的珍宝。**yond**:yonder.

29 **raisèd**:roused up.

30 **were best**:had better.　**must**:am destined to.

31 **parts**:personal qualities.　**perfect**:completely assured.

32 **manifest**:make clear,show.　**rightly**:right.

33 **Janus**:罗马神话中的两面神,正是伊阿古所信奉的神明。**no**:not.

34 **Lieutenant**:副将。

37 **haste-post-haste**:post-haste,with great speed.

38 **matter**:business.

39 **divine**:guess.

40 **heat**:urgency.　**galleys**:古代战船。

41 **sequent**:successive.

46 **about**:round the city.　**several**:separate.　**guests**:searching parties.

OTHELLO 'Tis well I am found by you:
I will but spend a word here in the house
And go with you. *Exit*
CASSIO Ancient, what makes he here?
IAGO
50 Faith, he tonight hath boarded a land carack:
If it prove lawful prize, he's made for ever.
CASSIO
I do not understand.
IAGO He's married.
CASSIO To who?
IAGO
Marry, to — Come, Captain, will you go?
Enter Othello
OTHELLO Have with you.
CASSIO
Here comes another troop to seek for you.
Enter Brabantio, Roderigo, with officers and torches
IAGO
55 It is Brabantio: General, be advised,
He comes to bad intent.
OTHELLO Holla, stand there.
RODERIGO
Signor, it is the Moor.
BRABANTIO Down with him, thief!
IAGO
You, Roderigo? Come, sir, I am for you.
OTHELLO
Keep up your bright swords, for the dew will rush them.
60 Good signor, you shall more command with years
Than with your weapons.
BRABANTIO
O thou foul thief! Where hast thou stowed my daughter?

48 but: only.

49 makes: does.

50 boarded: ①(海盗)登船抢劫;②交配。　**land carack**: ①large trading ship;②妓女。

51 lawful prize: ①合法财产;②合法娶妻。　**is made**: 发了大财,功成名就。

52 who: whom.

53 Marry: an oath meaning 'by the Virgin Mary'.　**Come**: 喂。**Have with you**: let's go.

54 troop: party.

55 be advised: take warning, be cautious,小心。

56 to: with.

58 I ... you: 我来和你斗剑。

59 Keep up: sheathe,收起。

60 with years: with your seniority.

62 stowed: put away, hidden,藏起来。

Damned as thou art, thou hast enchanted her:
For I'll refer me to all things of sense,
65 If she in chains of magic were not bound,
Whether a maid, so tender, fair, and happy,
So opposite to marriage that she shunned
The wealthy curlèd darlings of our nation,
Would ever have — t'incur a general mock —
70 Run from her guardage to the sooty bosom
Of such a thing as thou: to fear, not to delight.
Judge me the world, if 'tis not gross in sense
That thou hast practised on her with foul charms,
Abused her delicate youth with drugs or minerals
75 That weakens motion. I'll have't disputed on;
'Tis probable, and palpable to thinking:
I therefore apprehend, and do attach thee
For an abuser of the world, a practiser
Of arts inhibited, and out of warrant.
80 Lay hold upon him: if he do resist,
Subdue him, at his peril.

OTHELLO   Hold your hands,
Both you of my inclining and the rest.
Were it my cue to fight, I should have known it
Without a prompter. Where will you that I go
85 To answer this your charge?

BRABANTIO   To prison, till fit time
Of law and course of direct session
Call thee to answer.

OTHELLO   What if I do obey?
How may the Duke be therewith satisfied,
Whose messengers are here about my side,
90 Upon some present business of the state
To bring me to him?

OFFICER   'Tis true, most worthy signor:
The Duke's in council, and your noble self

ACT I SCENE II

63 Damned: 注定要下地狱的。　**enchanted**: 用妖术迷住了。

64 refer me to: submit my case to.　**things of sense**: creatures with common sense.

67 opposite: opposed.

68 curlèd: 蓄着卷发的。

69 t'incur ... mock: (为结果状语)遭世人讪笑。

70 guardage: guardianship, 受监护状态。

71 to fear: (a thing fit) to frighten.

72 Judge ... world: Let the world judge for me.　**gross in sense**: obvious.

73 practised: used, strategem.　**foul charms**: 恶毒的符咒。

74 minerals: poisons.

75 motion: sense.　**disputed on**: 在法庭上评一评。

76 palpable: obvious.

77 attach: arrest.

78 abuser: deceiver.

79 arts inhabited: prohibited magic.　**out of warrant**: illegal.

81 Subdue: 制服。　**Hold**: restrain, stop.

82 inclining: following, party.

83 cue: part, turn.

84 prompter: 台词提示者(cue 和 prompter 均为舞台用语)。　**will**: wish.

86 course of direct session: regular legal proceedings.

89 about: by.

90 present: urgent.

    I am sure is sent for.
BRABANTIO   How? The Duke in council?
    In this time of the night? Bring him away.
95 Mine's not an idle cause; the Duke himself,
    Or any of my brothers of the state,
    Cannot but feel this wrong as 'twere their own;
    For if such actions may have passage free,
    Bondslaves and pagans shall our statesmen be. *Exeunt*

SCENE III

I. iii   *The Duke and Senators sitting at a table; with lights and attendants*

DUKE

    There is no composition in these news
    That gives them credit.
FIRST SENATOR   Indeed they are disproportioned.
    My letters say a hundred and seven galleys.
DUKE

    And mine, a hundred and forty.
SECOND SENATOR   And mine two hundred;
5 But though they jump not on a just account —
    As in these cases where the aim reports
    'Tis oft with difference — yet do they all confirm
    A Turkish fleet, and bearing up to Cyprus.
DUKE

    Nay, it is possible enough to judgement;
10 I do not so secure me in the error,
    But the main article I do approve
    In fearful sense.
SAILOR(*without*)   What, ho! What, ho! What, ho!
FIRST OFFICER

    A messenger from the galleys.
        Enter Sailor

94 **In**: at.   **away**: along.
95 **idle**: trivial, worthless.
97 **as**: as if.
98 **passage free**: free course.
99 **Bondslaves**: 奴隶。   **pagans**: 异教徒。

I. iii

1 **composition**: consistency.
2 **disproportioned**: inconsistent.
5 **jump**: agree.   **just**: exact.
6 **aim**: conjecture.
8 **up to**: down on.
9 **to**: 后省略 make.
10 **so … error**: take such (false) comfort in the discrepancies.
11 **But**: that … not.   **article**: point.   **approve**: accept, perceive.
12 **fearful**: to be feared.

DUKE
                              Now, what's the business?
SAILOR
  The Turkish preparation makes for Rhodes;
15 So was I bid report here to the state
  By Signor Angelo.
DUKE
  How say you by this change?
FIRST SENATOR   This cannot be,
  By no assay of reason. 'Tis a pageant
  To keep us in false gaze. When we consider
20 Th'importancy of Cyprus to the Turk,
  And let ourselves again but understand
  That as it more concerns the Turk than Rhodes,
  So may he with more facile question bear it,
  For that it stands not in such warlike brace,
25 But altogether lacks th'abilities
  That Rhodes is dressed in. If we make thought of this,
  We must not think the Turk is so unskilful
  To leave that latest which concerns him first,
  Neglecting an attempt of ease and gain
30 To wake and wage a danger profitless.
DUKE
  Nay, in all confidence, he's not for Rhodes.
FIRST OFFICER
  Here is more news.

      Enter a Messenger

MESSENGER
  The Ottomites, reverend and gracious,
  Steering with due course toward the isle of Rhodes,
35 Have there injointed with an after fleet.
FIRST SENATOR
  Ay, so I thought. How many, as you guess?
MESSENGER
  Of thirty sail; and now they do re-stem

ACT I SCENE III

14 preparation: fleet prepared for battle.

15 bid report: bidden to report.

17 How say you by: what do you say about.　**cannot be**: i. e., cannot be a change.

18 assay: test.　**pageant**: show, feint, 假相。

19 in false gaze: looking the wrong way.

20 importancy: importance.

21 but: only.

22 it: i. e., Cyprus.

23 facile: easy.　**question**: trial by arms.　**bear**: capture.

24 For that: for, since.　**brace**: state of defence.

25 abilities: defence facilities.

26 dressed in: equipped with.　**make thought of**: consider.

27 unskilful: deficient in judgment.

28 that latest: i. e., Cyprus.

29 attempt: warlike enterprise.

30 wake: stir up.　**wage**: risk, venture.

31 in all confidence: we can be sure.

33 Ottomites: people of the Ottoman Empire, Turks, 土耳其人。 **reverend and gracious**: 公爵和各位大人, 此为插入的致敬语。

35 injointed: joined.　**after** (adj.): rear, 殿后的。

37 re-stem: steer again, retrace.

    Their backward course, bearing with frank appearance
    Their purposes toward Cyprus. Signor Montano,
    Your trusty and most valiant servitor,
    With his free duty recommends you thus,
    And prays you to believe him.

DUKE
    'Tis certain then for Cyprus.
    Marcus Luccicos, is not he in town?

FIRST SENATOR
    He's now in Florence.

DUKE   Write from us: wish him
    Post post-haste dispatch.

FIRST SENATOR
    Here comes Brabantio and the valiant Moor.

*Enter Brabantio, Othello, Iago, Roderigo,
and officers*

DUKE
    Valiant Othello, we must straight employ you
    Against the general enemy Ottoman.
    (*To Brabantio*) I did not see you: welcome, gentle signor;
    We lacked your counsel and your help tonight.

BRABANTIO
    So did I yours. Good your grace, pardon me:
    Neither my place, nor aught I heard of business,
    Hath raised me from my bed; nor doth the general care
    Take hold on me; for my particular grief
    Is of so flood-gate and o'erbearing nature
    That it engluts and swallows other sorrows
    And yet is still itself.

DUKE   Why? What's the matter?

BRABANTIO
    My daughter! O, my daughter!

SENATORS   Dead?

38　frank: open, undisguised, 毫不掩饰的。
40　servitor: 仆人。
41　free duty: unqualified expression of respect.　**recommends**: informs.
46　Post post-haste: hasty.　**dispatch**: speed, expedition.
48　straight(adv.): straightway.
49　general enemy: 公敌意指基督教世界(all Christendom)的公敌。　**Ottoman**: 奥托曼(即 Turkey),土耳其。
50　gentle: noble.
53　aught: anything.
55　particular: personal, private.
56　so: such.　**flood-gate**: torrential.　**o'erbearing**: 压倒一切的。
57　engluts: swallows up.

BRABANTIO   Ay, to me.
60   She is abused, stolen from me, and corrupted
       By spells and medicines bought of mountebanks;
       For nature so preposterously to err,
       Being not deficient, blind, or lame of sense,
       Sans witchcraft could not.

DUKE

65   Whoe'er he be that in this foul proceeding
       Hath thus beguiled your daughter of herself
       And you of her, the bloody book of law
       You shall yourself read in the bitter letter
       After your own sense, yea, though our proper son
70   Stood in your action.

BRABANTIO   Humbly I thank your grace.
       Here is the man; this Moor, whom now it seems
       Your special mandate for the state affairs
       Hath hither brought.

ALL   We are very sorry for't.

DUKE

       What in your own part can you say to this?

BRABANTIO

75   Nothing, but this is so.

OTHELLO

       Most potent, grave and reverend signors,
       My very noble and approved good masters,
       That I have ta'en away this old man's daughter,
       It is most true; true I have married her;
80   The very head and front of my offending
       Hath this extent, no more. Rude am I in my speech
       And little blessed with the soft phrase of peace;
       For since these arms of mine had seven years' pith
       Till now some nine moons wasted, they have used
85   Their dearest action in the tented field;
       And little of this great world can I speak

59　Ay [ai]: yes.

60　abused: deceived.

61　of: off.　**mountebanks**: 骗人的庸医（专指贩卖毒药和春药的人）。

62　nature: 人性（这里指 Desdemona 的性格）。　**err**: stray.

62—64 此句核心为 nature could not (to) err, 这里 could not 等于 was not able.

63　deficient: defective.　**lame**: imperfect.

64　Sans〈法语〉: without.

66　beguiled: deprived, robbed herself her reason.

67　bloody: cruel.

68　read: interpret.　**bitter**: sharp, severe.

69　After: according to.　**sense**: understanding.　**our proper**: my own. 旧时国王和公爵自称朕，英文用第一人称复数代词，称 royal we.

70　Stood in: was the object of.　**action**: lawsuit.　**your grace**: （对公爵的尊称）殿下。

72　mandate: order.

73　Hath: has 当时英格兰北方读音 has，南方读音 hath，莎氏混用。

74　in: on（此短语即 on your own behalf）.

76　potent: powerful.

77　approved: proved, esteemed.　**masters**: sirs, 先生们。

78　ta'en: taken, carried.

80　head and front: height and breadth, entire extent, 总体。

81　Rude: unpolished.

82　soft phrase: gentle words.

83—84　pith: strength, vigour.　**since … wasted**: 从我七岁起一直到九个月以前（过去九个月奥瑟罗待在威尼斯）。　**moons**: months.　**wasted**: gone by, elapsed.

85　tented field: battle field.　**dearest action**: at most exertion.

More than pertains to feats of broil and battle;
And therefore little shall I grace my cause
In speaking for myself. Yet, by your gracious patience,
90 I will a round unvarnished tale deliver
Of my whole course of love: what drugs, what charms,
What conjuration and what mighty magic —
For such proceedings I am charged withal —
I won his daughter.

BRABANTIO   A maiden never bold;
95 Of spirit so still and quiet that her motion
Blushed at herself; and she, in spite of nature,
Of years, of country, credit, everything,
To fall in love with what she feared to look on!
It is a judgement maimed and most imperfect
100 That will confess perfection so could err
Against all rules of nature, and must be driven
To find out practices of cunning hell
Why this should be. I therefore vouch again
That with some mixtures powerful o'er the blood,
105 Or with some dram conjured to this effect,
He wrought upon her.

DUKE   To vouch this is no proof,
Without more wider and more overt test
Than these thin habits and poor likelihoods
Of modern seeming do prefer against him.

FIRST SENATOR
110 But, Othello, speak:
Did you by indirect and forcèd courses
Subdue and poison this young maid's affections?
Or came it by request and such fair question
As soul to soul affordeth?

OTHELLO   I do beseech you,
115 Send for the lady to the Sagittary,
And let her speak of me before her father.

ACT I SCENE III

87　pertains to：relates to, 关于。　　**feats … battle**：战功。**broil**：quarrel, battle（broil 与 battle 为双声同义词，用 and 连接表示强调）。

88　grace：endow with graces, favour.

89　patience：indulgence, permission.

90　round：plain.　　**unvarnished**：without adornment.

91—92　my whole course of love：the whole course of my love. **what**：前省略 with, 四处皆同。

93　withal：with 本应在 such 之前，改置句尾则改为 withal.

95　motion：emotion, agitation.

97　years：i. e., difference in age.　　**credit**：reputation.

100　confess：Consede 后面省略 that.　　**perfection**：a perfect person（用抽象名词指具体的人的一种转喻，修辞学中称为 metonymy）。**so … err**：could go wrong in such a way.

101　must 的主语不明，可理解为 judgement，也可理解为省略掉 one.

102　practices：plots.

103　vouch：asserts.

104　mixtures：混合药物。　　**blood**：passions（中世纪欧洲人认为血为 seat of passion）。

105　dram：1/8 盎司剂量的药。　　**conjured**：influenced by a magic spell.

106　wrought：worked.

107　more wider：fuller（双重比较级）。　　**overt**：evident.

108　habits：garments, i. e. semblances.　　**likelihoods**：probabilities.

109　modern：commonplace.　　**seeming**：assumption.　　**prefer against**：bring a charge against, 指控。

111　forcèd：unnatural.

113　question：conversation.

If you do find me foul in her report,
The trust, the office I do hold of you
Not only take away, but let your sentence
120 Even fall upon my life.
DUKE   Fetch Desdemona hither.
OTHELLO
Ancient, conduct them: you best know the place.

Exit Iago with attendants

And till she come, as truly as to heaven
I do confess the vices of my blood,
So justly to your grave ears I'll present
125 How I did thrive in this fair lady's love,
And she in mine.
DUKE   Say it, Othello.
OTHELLO
Her father loved me, oft invited me,
Still questioned me the story of my life
From year to year — the battles, sieges, fortunes
130 That I have passed.
I ran it through, even from my boyish days
To th'very moment that he bade me tell it:
Wherein I spake of most disastrous chances,
Of moving accidents by flood and field,
135 Of hair-breadth scapes i'th'imminent deadly breach,
Of being taken by the insolent foe,
And sold to slavery; of my redemption thence,
And portance in my travels' history:
Wherein of antres vast and deserts idle,
140 Rough quarries, rocks, and hills whose heads touch heaven,
It was my hint to speak — such was the process:
And of the Cannibals that each other eat,
The Anthropophagi, and men whose heads
Do grow beneath their shoulders. This to hear

ACT I SCENE III

122 **as … heaven**: 对天盟誓。

123 **vices of my blood**: faults of my passion.

124 **justly**: exactly.　**grave**: dignified.

125 **thrive**: be successful.

127 **oft**: often.

128 **Still**: continually.　**questioned me**: inquired of me.

130 **passed**: experienced.

131 **ran it through**: told it all.

133 **chances**: events, occurrences.

134 **moving accidents**: exciting happenings.　**by … field**: by water and by land, 海上陆上 (flood and field 是双声)。

135 **scapes**: escapes.　**breach**: gap made in a fortification.

137 **thence**: i. e. from slavery.

138 **portance**: behaviour.

139 **antres** 〈法语〉: caves.　**idle**: barren, uninhabited.

141 **It … speak**: 这是我谈话的题目，speak 接 139 行的 of. **hint**: occasion, opportunity.　**process**: story, narrative.

142 **Cannibals**: 食人者。

143 **Anthropophagi**: man-eaters.

145 Would Desdemona seriously incline:
But still the house affairs would draw her thence,
Which ever as she could with haste dispatch
She'd come again, and with a greedy ear
Devour up my discourse; which I observing
150 Took once a pliant hour, and found good means
To draw from her a prayer of earnest heart
That I would all my pilgrimage dilate
Whereof by parcels she had something heard,
But not intentively. I did consent,
155 And often did beguile her of her tears
When I did speak of some distressful stroked
That my youth suffered. My story being done,
She gave me for my pains a world of sighs:
She swore, in faith 'twas strange, 'twas passing strange,
160 'Twas pitiful, 'twas wondrous pitiful;
She wished she had not heard it, yet she wished
That heaven had made her such a man. She thanke me,
And bade me, if I had a friend that loved her,
I should but teach him how to tell my story,
165 And that would woo her. Upon this hint I spake:
She loved me for the dangers I had passed,
And I loved her, that she did pity them.
This only is the witchcraft I have used.
Here comes the lady: let her witness it.

Enter Desdemona, Iago, and attendants

DUKE
170 I think this tale would win my daughter too.
Good Brabantio, take up this mangled matter at the best:
Men do their broken weapons rather use
Than their bare hands.
BRABANTIO   I pray you hear her speak.
If she confess that she was half the wooer,
175 Destruction on my head, if my bad blame

ACT I SCENE III

146　still: continually.

147　dispatch: do quickly.

148　She'd: She would.

150　pliant: suitable.　**hour**: time.

152　dilate: relate at length.

153　by parcels: by parts, piecemeal.

154　intentively: with full attention.

155　beguile … tears: coax tears from her.

156　stroke: accident.

158　for my pains: as reward.　**a world of**: 大量的(为夸张修辞格 hyperbole).

159　in faith: indeed.　**passing** (adv.): surpassingly, extremely.

160　wondrous (adv.): wonderfully.

163　bade: told.

164　but: only.

165　woo: win.　**spake**: spoke (of my love for her).

166　passed: experienced.

167　them: i.e. the dangers.

169　witness: give evidence of, testify to.

171　take … best: make the best of this mangled (bungled) business.

175　Destruction on my head: let destruction fall on my head.

Light on the man! Come hither, gentle mistress;
Do you perceive in all this company
Where most you owe obedience?
DESDEMONA   My noble father,
I do perceive here a divided duty:
180 To you I am bound for life and education;
My life and education both do learn me
How to respect you. You are lord of all my duty,
I am hitherto your daughter. But here's my husband;
And so much duty as my mother showed
185 To you, preferring you before her father,
So much I challenge, that I may profess
Due to the Moor, my lord.
BRABANTIO   God bu'y! I have done.
Please it your grace, on to the state affairs.
I had rather to adopt a child than get it.
190 Come hither, Moor:
I here do give thee that with all my heart
Which, but thou hast already, with all my heart
I would keep from thee. For your sake, jewel,
I am glad at soul I have no other child,
195 For thy escape would teach me tyranny
To hang clogs on them. I have done, my lord.
DUKE
Let me speak like yourself and lay a sentence
Which as a grise or step may help these lovers
Into your favour.
200 When remedies are past the griefs are ended
By seeing the worst which late on hopes depended.
To mourn a mischief that is past and gone
Is the next way to draw new mischief on.
What cannot be preserved when fortune takes,
205 Patience her injury a mockery makes.
The robbed that smiles steals something from thief;

176 **mistress**: 对女子的一般称呼,这里是父对女。

186 **challenge**: claim 其宾语为 so much,及其同位语 that 引导的从句。

187 **God bu'y**: God by with you. **I … done**: 我没说的了。

188 **Please it**: if it please. **on**: 前面省略 go.

189 **had rather to**: had rather 后的不定式动词现在已省略 to.

191—192 **that … Which**: i. e., my daughter.

192 **but**: if not for the fact that.

193 **For … sake**: on your account.

194 **at soul**: at heart.

195 **escape**: elopement.

196 **hang clogs on**: 旧时在牛马腿上拴笨重的木块(clogs),使它们不致走失。此处为借喻。

197 **like yourself**: as you would. **lay**: put forward. **sentence**: maxim.

198 **grise**: gree, degree, step (grise 和 step 在这里为成对的同义词)。

200 **remedies**: hopes of remedy. 请注意从此行开始至 217 行用双行一韵的诗体(couplets).

201 **late**(adv.): lately. **on hopes depended**: (the griefs) were sustained by hopeful anticipation.

202 **mischief**: misfortune.

203 **next**: nearest.

204 **What**: whatever. **takes**: 夺走。

205 **Patience … makes**: Patience makes a mockery of Fortune's injury. 此处将 Patience 和 Fortune 都拟人化了。

>   He robs himself that spends a bootless grief.
>
> BRABANTIO
>
>   So let the Turk of Cyprus us beguile,
>   We lose it not so long as we can smile;
> 210 He bears the sentence well that nothing bears
>   But the free comfort which from thence he hears;
>   But he bears both the sentence and the sorrow
>   That to pay grief must of poor patience borrow.
>   These sentences, to sugar or to gall
> 215 Being strong on both sides, are equivocal.
>   But words are words; I never yet did hear
>   That the bruised heart was piecèd through the ear.
>   I humbly beseech you proceed to th'affairs of state.
>
> DUKE The Turk with a most mighty preparation makes
> 220 for Cyprus. Othello, the fortitude of the place is best
>   known to you: and though we have there a substitute
>   of most allowed sufficiency, yet opinion, a more sover-
>   eign mistress of effects, throws a more safer voice on
>   you. You must therefore be content to slubber the gloss
> 225 of your new fortunes with this more stubborn and bois-
>   terous expedition.
>
> OTHELLO
>
>   The tyrant, custom, most grave Senators,
>   Hath made the flinty and steel couch of war
>   My thrice-driven bed of down. I do agnize
> 230 A natural and prompt alacrity
>   I find in hardness; and do undertake
>   This present war against the Ottomites.
>   Most humbly, therefore, bending to your state,
>   I crave fit disposition for my wife,
> 235 Due refernece of place and exhibition,
>   With such accommodation and besort
>   As levels with her breeding.
>
> DUKE   If you please,

ACT I SCENE III

207 spends: gives vent to. **bootless**: useless.
208 us beguile: rob us (of Cyprus).
210 连续几行中的 **sentence**: ①maxim; ②judicial sentence, 双关的文字游戏。
210—211 A person well bears out your maxim (well endures the judicial sentence) who takes with him nothing except the philosophic consolation which he learns from it.
212—213 But a person will suffer both the sentence and the sorrow who must borrow from her patience.
214 sugar: sweetness. **gall**: bitterness.
215 strong: resistant. **equivocal**: 模棱两可的。
217 piecèd: pieced together, 拼合复原。在此情况下, though the ear 的意思为"靠听到的劝告"。另一版本此字为 pierced, 意思是 Surgically lanced and cured (through the ear).
219—226 散文体。
220 fortitude: physical or structural strengh.
221 substitute: deputy.
222—223 allowed sufficiency: acknowledged ability. **opinion**: general judgement. **sovereigna**: authoritative.
223 effects: affairs. **more safer**: 双重比较级, more reliable. **voice**: reputation.
224 slubber: soil, sull, 玷污, 弄暗。
225—226 new fortunes: 新的好运（指新婚）。 **stubborn and boisterous**: tough and violent.
227 custom: 习惯（被拟人化为 tyrant 暴君）, 这里作 tyrant 的同位语。
229 thrice-driven: winnowed by currents of air driven three times through the down (鸭毛)。 **agnize**: acknowledge.
230 alacrity: readiness, eagerness.
231 in hardness: in accepting hardship.
233 bending ... state: bowing to your high dignity.
234 crave for: beg for. **fit disposition**: proper arrangement.
235 exhibition: financial provision, allowance, 津贴。 **reference**: assignment.
236 accommodation: supply of conveniences. **besort**: suitable company.
237 levels: equals, suits. **breeding**: birth. **If ... please**: if you like.

Be't at her father's.

BRABANTIO I'll not have it so.

OTHELLO
  Nor I.

DESDEMONA Nor I: I would not there reside
240 To put my father in impatient thoughts
By being in his eye. Most gracious Duke,
To my unfolding lend your prosperous ear,
And let me find a charter in your voice
T'assist my simpleness.

DUKE What would you? Speak.

DESDEMONA
245 That I did love the Moor to live with him,
My downright violence and storm of fortunes
May trumpet to the world. My heart's subdued
Even to the very quality of my lord.
I saw Othello's visage in his mind,
250 And to his honours and his valiant parts
Did I my soul and fortunes consecrate.
So that, dear lords, if I be left behind
A moth of peace, and he go to the war,
The rites for which I love him are bereft me,
255 And I a heavy interim shall support
By his dear absence. Let me go with him.

OTHELLO
  Let her have your voice.
  Vouch with me, heaven, I therefore beg it not
  To please the palate of my appetite,
260 Nor to comply with heat — the young affects
  In me defunct — and proper satisfaction;
  But to be free and bounteous to her mind.
  And heaven defend your good souls that you think
  I will your serious and great business scant
265 For she is with me. No, when light-winged toys

ACT I SCENE III

240 impatient: fretful.

241 eye: sight, view.

242 unfolding: disclosure, explanation. **prosperous**: propitious, favourable.

243 charter: authorization.

244 assist: support. **simpleness**: innocence, simple request. **What would you?**: What do you wish?

245 to: in order to.

246 violence and storm of fortunes: violent and stormy fortunes.

247 trumpet (v. t.): publish, declare(此句核心为 my fortunes may trumpet that …). **subdued**: submitted, subservient.

248 quality: character, disposition.

249 visage: face, i. e., Desdemona valued Othello's mind more than his face.

250—251 I consecrated my soul and fortunes to his honours and his valiant parts. **parts**: abilities, qualities. **consecrate**: dedicate, devote.

252 So that: therefore.

253 moth of peace: a peace-time parasite.

254 rites: i. e., those of marriage and love. **bereft** (p. p.): of bereave, deprive, rob.

255 heavy interim: sorrowful interval of time. **shall**: shall have to. **support**: endure.

256 By: because of. **his dear absence**: the absence of him who is dear.

257 voice: support, approval.

260 comply with: satisfy. **heat**: lust. **affects**: passions, desires.

262 free: generous. **bounteous**: liberal.

263 defend: forbid, prevent. **think**: should think that.

264 will: would. **scant** (v. t.): neglect.

265 For: because. **light-winged toys**: trivial matters, trifling delights.

            Of feathered Cupid seel with wanton dullness
            My speculative and officed instruments,
            That my disports corrupt and taint my business,
            Let housewives make a skillet of my helm,
270   And all indign and base adversities
            Make head against my estimation!
      DUKE
            Be it as you shall privately determine,
            Either for her stay, or going. Th'affair cries haste,
            And speed must answer it. You must hence tonight.
      DESDEMONA
275   Tonight, my lord?
      DUKE   This night.
      OTHELLO   With all my heart.
      DUKE
            At nine i'th'morning, here we'll meet again.
            Othello, leave some officer behind,
            And he shall our commission bring to you,
            With such things else of quality and respect
280   As doth import you.
      OTHELLO   So please your grace, my Ancient.
            A man he is of honesty and trust;
            To his conveyance I assign my wife,
            With what else needful your good grace shall think
            To be sent after me.
      DUKE   Let it be so.
285   Good night to everyone. And, noble signor,
            If virtue no delighted beauty lack,
            Your son-in-law is far more fair than black.
      FIRST SENATOR
            Adieu, brave Moor; use Desdemona well.
      BRABANTIO
            Look to her, Moor, if thou hast eyes to see.
290   She has deceived her father, and may thee.

266 Cupid：丘比特(罗马神话中长翅膀的小爱神)。　　**seel**(v. t.)：blind. 驯猎鹰时将鹰眼皮用线缝住使看不见,叫做 seel.　**wanton**：纵欲的,放任的。　　**dullness**：drowsiness.

267　**speculative … instruments**：powers of sights and official action.

268　**That**：so that.　　**disports**：amusements.

269　**skillet**：saucepan,长把儿小锅。　　**helm**：helmet,头盔。

270　**indign**：unworthy.

271　**Make head against**：attack.　　**estimation**：reputation.

273　**cries**：calls for.

274　**hence**：from here 前面省略 go.

278　**commission**：formal document of appointment,委任状。

280　**import** (v. t.)：concern.

282　**conveyance**：escort.　**assign**：consign, entrust.

286　**delighted**：delightful.

287　**fair**：原意为白皮肤,转义为美丽。

288　**use**：treat.

289　**Look to**：watch over.

OTHELLO
My life upon her faith!
Exeunt Duke, Senators, and attendants
Honest Iago,
My Desdemona must I leave to thee.
I prithee let thy wife attend on her,
And bring them after in the best advantage.
295 Come, Desdemona, I have but an hour
Of love, of worldly matters and direction
To spend with thee. We must obey the time.
Exeunt Othello and Desdemona

RODERIGO Iago.

IAGO What say'st thou, noble heart?

300 RODERIGO What will I do, think'st thou?

IAGO Why, go to bed and sleep.

RODERIGO I will incontinently drown myself.

IAGO If thou dost, I shall never love thee after. Why, thou silly gentleman!

305 RODERIGO It is silliness to live, when to live is torment: and then we have a prescription to die, when death is our physician.

IAGO O villainous! I have looked upon the world for four times seven years, and since I could distinguish betwixt
310 a benefit and an injury, I never found a man that knew how to love himself. Ere I would say I would drown myself for the love of a guinea-hen, I would change my humanity with a baboon.

RODERIGO What should I do? I confess it is my shame to
315 be so fond, but it is not in my virtue to amend it.

IAGO Virtue? A fig! 'Tis in ourselves that we are thus, or thus. Our bodies are our gardens, to the which our wills are gardeners. So that if we will plant nettles or sow lettuce, set hyssop and weed up thyme, supply it
320 with one gender of herbs or distract it with many, ether

ACT I SCENE III

291 我以生命担保她是忠诚的。

293 **prithee**：pray you.

294 **in ... advantage**：at the best opportunity.

300 **will**：shall.

302 **incontinently**：immediately.

306 **prescription**：药方。

311 **Ere**：before.

312 **guinea-hen**：雌珍珠鸡，俚语中转义妓女。

313 **baboon**：狒狒。

315 **fond**：foolishly loving. **virtue**：power.

316 **A fig**：nonsense 原意为无花果，微不足道之物。下等社会风俗，把拇指夹在二三指间示人的一种侮辱性手势，也叫 to give a fig.

317 **to the which**：to which. which 原为名词，故可加冠词。**wills**：will 旧时抽象名词可有复数。

319 **set**：栽种。 **hyssop**：海索草（一种有香味的春药）。**thyme**：百里香。

320 **gender**：kind. **distract it with**：divide it among.

to have it sterile with idleness or manured with industry, why the power and corrigible authority of this lies in our wills. If the beam of our lives had not one scale of reason to poise another of sensuality, the blood and baseness of our natures would conduct us to most preposterous conclusions. But we have reason to cool our raging motions, our carnal stings, our unbitted lusts; where of I take this, that you call love, to be a sect or scion.

RODERIGO It cannot be.

IAGO It is merely a lust of the blood and a permission of the will. Come, be a man. Drown thyself? Drown cats and blind puppies. I have professed me thy friend, and I confess me kint to thy deserving with cables perdurable toughness. I could never better stead thee than now. Put money in thy purse. Follow thou these wars; defeat thy favour with an usurped beard. I say, put money in thy purse. It cannot be that Desdemona should long continue her love to the Moor — put money in thy purse — nor he his to her. It was a violent commencement, and thou shalt see an answerable sequestration — put but money in thy purse. These Moors are changeable in their wills — fill thy purse with money. The food that to him now is as luscious as locusts shall be to him shortly as acerbe as the coloquintida. She must change for youth; when she is sated with his body she will find the error of her choice. Therefore put money in thy purse. If thou wilt needs damn thyself, do it a more delicate way than drowning. Make all the money thou canst. If sanctimony and a frail vow betwixt an erring barbarian and a super-subtle Venetian be not too hard for my wits and all the tribe of hell, thou shalt enjoy her — therefore make money. A pox of drowning thyself? It is clean out of the way. Seek

321 **idleness**: want of cultivation.

322 **why**: 语气词。 **corrigible authority**: corrective power.

323 **beam**: 天平的横杆,秤杆。 **scale**: 天平的盘子。

324—325 **poise**: counterbalance. **blood and baseness**: animal instincts.

325 **conduct**: lead.

327 **raging**: violent. **motions**: appetites, desires. **carnal stings**: sexual desires. **unbitted**: uncontrolled, unbridled. bit 原意为马上嚼子。

328 **where of**: of which (lusts). **take**: understand. **sect**: cutting.

329 **scion**: offshoot.

331 **It**: i. e., "What you call love."

334 **knit** (p. p.): knitted, tied. **thy deserving**: what you deserve. **perdurable**: endurable, long-lasting.

335 **stead** (v. t.): help, benefit.

337 **defeat**: disguise. **favour**: face. **an usurped**: a false.

340 **he his**: he should continue his love.

341 **answerable**: corresponding. **sequestration**: separation.

342 **but**: only.

344 **luscious**: delicious. **locusts**: locust-beans, fruits of the carob tree,角豆树的果实,味甜。

345 **shortly**: soon. **acerbe**: sour and bitter. **coloquintida**: 药西瓜,味苦。

346 **for**: because of. **sated**: satiated, fed up.

349 **Make**: raise, collect.

350 **sanctimony**: i. e., sacred marriage bond.

351 **erring**: wandering. **super-subtle**: most delicate.

352 **tribe of hell**: i. e., devils.

353 **pox**: plague.

354 **of**: on. a pox on 为诅咒语。 **clean** (adv.): completely. **out of the way**: out of place, inappropriate.

355 thou rather to be hanged in compassing thy joy than to
be drowned and go without her.

RODERIGO Wilt thou be fast to my hopes, if I depend on
the issue?

IAGO Thou art sure of me. Go make money. I have told
360 thee often, and I re-tell thee again and again, I hate the
Moor. My cause is hearted: thine hath no less reason.
Let us be conjunctive in our revenge against him. If
thou canst cuckold him, thou dost thyself a pleasure,
me a sport. There are many events in the womb of time,
365 which will be delivered. Traverse! Go, provide thy
money. We will have more of this tomorrow. Adieu.

RODERIGO Where shall we meet i'th'morning?

IAGO At my lodging.

370 RODERIGO I'll be with thee betimes.

IAGO Go to; farewell. Do you hear, Roderigo?

RODERIGO What say you?

IAGO No more of drowning, do you hear?

RODERIGO I am changed.

375 IAGO Go to; farewell. Put money enough in your purse.

RODERIGO I'll sell all my land.   *Exit*

IAGO

  Thus do I ever make my fool my purse:
  For I mine own gained knowledge should profane
  If I would time expend with such a snipe
380 But for my sport and profit. I hate the Moor,
  And it is thought abroad that 'twixt my sheets
  He's done my office. I know not if't be true
  But I, for mere suspicion in that kind,
  Will do as if for surety. He holds me well:
385 The better shall my purpose work on him.
  Cassio's a proper man: let me see now;
  To get his place and to plume up my will
  In double knavery. How? How? Let's see.

355 compassing: encompassing, bringing about.

356 go: depart, die.

357 fast: firmly, adhering.

358 issue: result, outcome.

359 art sure: can be sure.

361 hearted: heart-felt.

362 conjunctive: united.

363 cuckold: 使戴绿帽子,此字源于 cuckoo,杜鹃鸟惯于在其他鸟的巢中生蛋,与有夫之妇通奸为 cuckold 丈夫。 **dost**: render, give.

364 sport: amusement.

365 Traverse: march(军事口令)。

370 betimes: early.

374 I am changed: I have changed my mind.

378 profane: insult.

379 expend: spend. **snipe**: woodcock,山鹬,呆鸟,i. e., fool.

381—382 thought abroad: rumoured. **'twixt ... office**: seduced my wife. **office**: work, job.

383 kind: manner, way.

384 He ... well: He esteems me.

386 proper: handsome.

387 plume up: adorn with feather, crown with success.

>   After some time, to abuse Othello's ear
> 390 That he is too familiar with his wife;
>   He hath a person and a smooth dispose
>   To be suspected, framed to make women false.
>   The Moor is of a free and open nature,
>   That thinks men honest that but seem to be so,
> 395 And will as tenderly be led by th'nose
>   As asses are.
>   I have't. It is engendered. Hell and night
>   Must bring this monstrous birth to the world's light.
>   *Exit*

389 abuse: impose on, deceive.

390 he: i.e., Cassio.　**his**: i.e., Othello's.

391—392 He ... suspected: Cassio is handsome and has an easy disposition that is apt to rouse suspicion.

392 framed: formed, shaped.

393 free: frank.　**open**: unsuspicious.

394 that: so that he.　**but**: only.

395 tenderly: easily.

397 engendered: conceived.

398 birth: offering 指伊阿古心中所怀的罪恶计划将会出台。

ACT II

SCENE I

II. i *Enter Montano and two Gentlemen*

MONTANO

What from the cape can you discern at sea?

FIRST GENTLEMAN

Nothing at all; it is a high-wrought flood.
I cannot 'twixt the heaven and the main
Descry a sail.

MONTANO

5 Methinks the wind does speak aloud at land;
A fuller blast ne'er shook our battlements.
If it hath ruffianed so upon the sea,
What ribs of oak, when mountains melt on them,
Can hold the mortise? What shall we hear of this?

SECOND GENTLEMAN

10 A segregation of the Turkish fleet;
For do but stand upon the banning shore,
The chidden billow seems to pelt the clouds;
The wind-shaked surge, with high and monstrous mane,
Seems to cast water on the burning Bear
15 And quench the guards of th'ever-fixèd Pole.
I never did like molestation view
On the enchafèd flood.

MONTANO   If that the Turkish fleet
Be not ensheltered and embayed, they are drowned;
It is impossible they bear it out.

Enter a Gentleman

THIRD GENTLEMAN

II. i

   2 **high-wrought**: highly agitated, stormy.

   3 **main**: sea.

   4 **Descry**: see.

   5 **Methinks**: it seems to me. **speak**: make noise.

   7 **ruffianed**: acted like a ruffian, raged. **so**: likewise.

   8 **ribs of oak**: 用橡木做船的肋材。 **mountains**: mountainous waves. **melt**: stream, sweep.

   9 **mortise**: 榫头。

  10 **segregation**: scattering, dispersal.

  11 **banning**: repelling the advancing waves. 此字在另一版本中为 foaming.

  12 **chidden**: rebuked, repelled. **pelt**: assail.

  13 **shaked**: shaken. **mane**: 马鬃用以喻浪头之泡沫。

  14 **Bear**: Great Bear, 大熊星座。

  15 **guards … Pole**: 小熊星座(the Little Bear)的两颗星被认为是北极星的守卫星。

  16 **like**: comparable. **molestation**: disturbance. **view**: see.

  17 **enchafèd**: agitated, stormy. **If that**: if.

  18 **ensheltered**: sheltered. **embayed**: brought to bay landlocked. **are drowned**: are bound to be shipwrecked.

  19 **bear it out**: withstand or survive the storm.

20 News, lads! Our wars are done;
    The desperate tempest hath so banged the Turks
    That their designment halts. A noble ship of Venice
    Hath seen a grievous wrack and sufferance
    On most part of their fleet.

MONTANO

25 How! Is this true?

THIRD GENTLEMAN The ship is here put in,
    A Veronesa; Michael Cassio,
    Lieutenant to the warlike Moor, Othello,
    Is come on shore; the Moor himself at sea,
    And is in full commission here for Cyprus.

MONTANO

30 I am glad on't; 'tis a worthy governor.

THIRD GENTLEMAN

    But this same Cassio, though he speak of comfort
    Touching the Turkish loss, yet he looks sadly
    And prays the Moor be safe; for they were parted
    With foul and violent tempest.

MONTANO   Pray heaven he be;

35 For I have served him, and the man commands
    Like a full soldier. Let's to the sea-side, ho!
    As well to see the vessel that's come in,
    As to throw out our eyes for brave Othello,
    Even till we make the main and th'aerial blue
40 An indistinct regard.

THIRD GENTLEMAN Come, let's do so;
    For every minute is expectancy
    Of more arrivance.

        Enter Cassio

CASSIO

    Thanks, you the valiant of this warlike isle
    That so approve the Moor! O, let the heavens
45 Give him defence against the elements,

21　**banged**: knocked up.
22　**designment**: design, plan.　　**halts**: is crippled.　　**noble**: excellent.
23　**grievous … sufferance**: a severe wrecking and disaster.
24　**most**: 前省略 the.
27　**Veronesa**: 在 Verona 修造的船。
29　**in … commission**: with full powers, in full command.
30　**on't**: of it.
32　**Touching**: about.　　**sadly**: gravely.
34　**With**: by.　　**be**: i. e., be safe.
36　**full**: perfect.　　**to**: go to.
37—38　**As well … As**: both … and.
38　**throw out our eyes**: cast a look, watch out.
39　**th'aerial blue**: the sky.
40　**indistinct**: undistinguishable.　　**regard**: view.
41　**expectancy**: expectation.
42　**more arrivance**: the arrival of more ships.
44　**approve**: praise.
45　**elements**: the wind and the waves.

For I have lost him on a dangerous sea.

MONTANO

Is he well shipped?

CASSIO

His bark is stoutly timbered, and his pilot
Of very expert and approved allowance;
50 Therefore my hopes, not surfeited to death,
Stand in bold cure.

>   (*Cry within* 'A sail, a sail, a sail!')

CASSIO

What noise?

FOURTH GENTLEMAN

The town is empty; on the brow o'th'sea
Stand ranks of people, and they cry 'A sail!'

CASSIO

55 My hopes do shape him for the Governor.

>   *Salvo*

SECOND GENTLEMAN

They do discharge their shot of courtesy:
Our friends at least.

CASSIO   I pray you, sir, go forth,
And give us truth who 'tis that is arrived.

SECOND GENTLEMAN

I shall.   *Exit*

MONTANO

60 But, good Lieutenant, is your General wived?

CASSIO

Most fortunately: he hath achieved a maid
That paragons description and wild fame;
One that excels the quirks of blazoning pens,
And in th'essential vesture of creation
65 Does tire the ingener.

>   *Enter Second Gentleman*

How now? Who has put in?

47 Is ... shipped: Is his ship well-built?

49 approved allowance: tested reputation.

50 surfeited to death: over-extended.

51 Stand ... cure: have an excellent chance of fulfillment (hopes 拟人化,death 和 cure 指其健康状况)。

53 brow: edge.

55 shape: imagine, picture.　**Salvo**: firing of a number of guns together in salute.

58 is arrived: has arrived. 旧时凡运动动词多有此用法。

61 achieved: won.

62 paragons(v.): surpasses.　**wild fame**: extravagant report.

63 quirks: witty turns of expression.　**blazoning**: describing in heraldic or flattering terms.

64 essential: real.　**vesture of creation**: natural beauty 天生的(灵魂的)外衣。

65 tire: cause to tire, weary.　**ingener**: ingenious artist or poet. **put in**: i.e., to habour.

SECOND GENTLEMAN
> 'Tis one Iago, Ancient to the General.

CASSIO
> He's had most favourable and happy speed:
> Tempests themselves, high seas, and howling winds,
> The guttered rocks and congregated sands,
> 70 Traitors ensteeped to clog the guiltless keel,
> As having sense of beauty, do omit
> Their mortal natures, letting go safely by
> The divine Desdemona.

MONTANO What is she?

CASSIO
> She that I spake of, our great Captain's Captain,
> 75 Left in the conduct of the bold Iago,
> Whose footing here anticipates our thoughts
> A se'nnight's speed. Great Jove, Othello guard,
> And swell his sail with thine own powerful breath,
> That he may bless this bay with his tall ship,
> 80 Make love's quick pants in Desdemona's arms,
> Give renewed fire to our extincted spirits,
> And bring all Cyprus comfort.

> *Enter Desdemona, Emilia, Iago, Roderigo, and attendants*

> O, behold,
> The riches of the ship is come on shore!
> You men of Cyprus, let her have your knees.
> 85 Hail to thee, lady! And the grace of heaven,
> Before, behind thee, and on every hand,
> Enwheel thee round.

DESDEMONA I thank you, valiant Cassio.
> What tidings can you tell me of my lord?

CASSIO
> He is not yet arrived; nor know I aught
> 90 But that he's well, and will be shortly here.

69 guttered: jagged, hollowed. **congregated**: assembled.

70 ensteeped: submerged in water. **clog**: obstruct. **guiltless**: innocent, unaware.

71 As: as if. **having sense of beauty**: being sensitive to (Desdemona's) beauty. **omit**: let go, forbear.

72 mortal: deadly.

74 spake: spoke.

75 conduct: escort.

76 footing: landing. **anticipates**: forestalls, precedes. **thoughts**: idea, expectation.

77 A: 前省略 by. **se'nnight's**: seven nights', week's. **Jove**: 罗马神话中的主神,又名 Jupiter. **Othello guard**: pray guard Othello.

79 That: so that. **tall**: splendid.

81 extincted: extinguished.

83 is come: 参看前 58 行注,riches 视为单数。

84 let her have your knees: kneel before her.

85 And: 后省略 may.

87 Enwheel: encompass, encircle.

89 aught: anything.

90 But: except.

DESDEMONA

O, but I fear! How lost you company?

CASSIO

The great contention of the sea and skies
Parted our fellowship.

(*Cry within*) 'A sail, a sail!'

But hark, a sail!

GENTLEMAN

They give their greeting to the citadel:
95   This likewise is a friend.

CASSIO   See for the news.

Good Ancient, you are welcome. Welcome, mistress.
He kisses Emilia
Let it not gall your patience, good Iago,
That I extend my manners. 'Tis my breeding
That gives me this bold show of courtesy.

IAGO

100 Sir, would she give you so much of her lips
As of her tongue she oft bestows on me,
You'd have enough.

DESDEMONA

Alas, she has no speech.

IAGO   In faith, too much.

I find it still when I have list to sleep.
105 Marry, before your ladyship, I grant
She puts her tongue a little in her heart
And chides with thinking.

EMILIA   You have little cause to say so.

IAGO Come on, come on; you are pictures out of doors,
bells in your parlours, wild-cats in your kitchens, saints
110 in your injuries, devils being offended, players in your
housewifery, and housewives in your beds.

DESDEMONA

O, fie upon thee, slanderer!

ACT II SCENE I

91 **lost you company**: did you part from each other.
92 **contention**: conflict.
93 **hark**: listen.
94 **citadel**: 战船上的炮台。
97 **gall**: make sore, irritate.
98 **extend ... manners**: extend my courtesy (to your wife).
100 **would she**: if she should.
104 **still**: always.   **list**: desire.
105 **Marry**: by Virgin Mary.
107 **with thinking**: i.e., without words.
108 **pictures**: painted creatures, i.e. silent and well-behaved.
109—110 **bells**: noisy, ever jangling.   **saints ... injuries**: pretending to be saints when you hurt others.
110 **devils ... offended**: devils when you are offended.
111 **housewifery**: housekeeping.   **housewives**: hussies, 荡妇。
112 **fie upon thee**: 呸, 去你的。

IAGO
> Nay, it is true, or else I am a Turk:
> You rise to play and go to bed to work.

EMILIA
> You shall not write my praise.

IAGO   No, let me not.

DESDEMONA
> What wouldst thou write of me, if thou shouldst praise me?

IAGO
> O, gentle lady, do not put me to't,
> For I am nothing if not critical.

DESDEMONA
> Come on, assay. There's one gone to the harbour?

IAGO
> Ay, madam.

DESDEMONA
> (*aside*) I am not merry, but I do beguile
> The thing I am by seeming otherwise.
> Come, how wouldst thou praise me?

IAGO
> I am about it, but indeed my invention
> Comes from my pate as birdlime does from frieze —
> It plucks out brains and all. But my muse labours,
> And thus she is delivered.
> If she be fair and wise, fairness and wit,
> The one's for use, the other useth it.

DESDEMONA
> Well praised! How if she be black and witty?

IAGO
> If she be black, and thereto have a wit,
> She'll find a white that shall her blackness fit.

DESDEMONA
> Worse and worse.

114 **rise**: get up.

119 **assay**: try.

121 **beguile**: disguise.

124 **about it**: thinking about it.

125 **pate**: head.　**birdlime**: 粘鸟用的胶。　**frieze**: 起绒粗呢。

126 **muse**: 希腊神话中的文艺女神,传说每个诗人都有他自己的诗神。　**labours**: 分娩之阵痛。

127 **is delivered**: 生出孩子。

128—154 此处调侃斗智的俏皮话或用双韵句,或用白话散文。

129 **The one**: i. e. , fairness, beauty.　**the other**: wit, intelligence, cleverness.

130 **black and witty**: 黑丑而聪明。

132 **white**: a pun on "wight", meaning "person".

EMILIA How if fair and foolish?

IAGO

    She never yet was foolish that was fair,
135 For even her folly helped her to an heir.

DESDEMONA These are old fond paradoxes to make fools laugh i'th'alehouse. What miserable praise hast thou for her that's foul and foolish?

IAGO

    There's none so foul and foolish thereunto,
140 But does foul pranks which fair and wise ones do.

DESDEMONA O heavy ignorance! Thou praisest the worst best. But what praise couldst thou bestow on a deserving woman indeed? One that in the authority of her merit did justly put on the vouch of very malice itself?

IAGO

145 She that was ever fair and never proud,
    Had tongue at will, and yet was never loud;
    Never lacked gold, and yet went never gay;
    Fled from her wish, and yet said 'Now I may';
    She that being angered, her revenge being nigh,
150 Bade her wrong stay, and her displeasure fly;
    She that in wisdom never was so frail
    To change the cod's head for the salmon's tail;
    She that could think and ne'er disclose her mind;
    See suitors following and not look behind;
155 She was a wight, if ever such wight were —

DESDEMONA

    To do what?

IAGO

    To suckle fools and chronicle small beer.

DESDEMONA

    O, most lame and impotent conclusion!
    Do not learn of him, Emilia, though he be thy husband.
160 How say you, Cassio, is he not a most profane and

135 folly: ①foolishness; ②wantonness. **to an heir**: i. e. to bear a child.

136 food paradoxes: foolish self-contradictory remarks, 自相矛盾或似是而非的蠢话。

138 foul: ugly.

139 thereunto: pertaining to it, for it.

140 foul: dirty, sluttish. **pranks**: wanton actions, 放荡的行为。

141 heavy: dull, stupid.

143 in the authority of: on the strength of.

144 put on: compel. **vouch**: approval. **malice**: 拟人化, a malicious person.

147 gay: loose, dissipated.

148 wish: desire.

149 nigh: near, at hand.

150 wrong: sense of being wronged. **stay**: stop.

152 To: as to. **change … tail**: to exchange a foolish husband for a handsome lover.

155 wight: person. **were**: 前面省略 there.

157 suckle: breast feed. **chronicle**: account of.

159 learn of: learn from, listen to.

160 profane: coarse in language.

liberal counsellor?

CASSIO He speaks home, madam; you may relish him more in the soldier than in the scholar.

IAGO (*aside*) He takes her by the palm. Ay, well said, whisper. With as little a web as this will I ensnare as great a fly as Cassio. Ay, smile upon her, do. I will gyve thee in thine own courtship. You say true, 'tis so indeed. If such tricks as these strip you out of your lieutenantry, it had been better you had not kissed your three fingers so oft, which now again you are most apt to play the sir in. Very good; well kissed, an excellent courtesy! 'Tis so indeed. Yet again your fingers to your lips? Would they were clyster-pipes for your sake!

Trumpet

(*aloud*) The Moor! I know his trumpet.

CASSIO   'Tis truly so.

DESDEMONA

Let's meet him and receive him.

CASSIO   Lo, where he comes!

Enter Othello and attendants

OTHELLO

O, my fair warrior!

DESDEMONA   My dear Othello!

OTHELLO

It gives me wonder great as my content
To see you here before me. O, my soul's joy!
If after every tempest come such calms,
May the winds blow till they have wakened death,
And let the labouring bark climb hills of seas,
Olympus-high, and duck again as low
As hell's from heaven. If it were now to die,
'Twere now to be most happy; for I fear
My soul hath her content so absolute

161　liberal: free in speech.

162　home (adv.): plainly, to the point.　**relish**: appreciate.

163　in: in the character of.

164　well said: well done.

167　gyve: fetter, shackle.　**courtship**: show of courtly behaviour.

168　out of: of.

171　sir: fine gentleman.

173　clyster-pipes：灌肠用的管子。

177　great as: as great as.

182　Olympus-high: as high as Mount Olympus，希腊神话中诸神居住的高山。　**duck**: dive.

183　hell's: hell is.　**If … die**: if I were to die now.

184　'Twere: It would be.

That not another comfort like to this
Succeeds in unknown fate.

DESDEMONA   The heavens forbid-
But that our loves and comforts should increase,
Even as our days do grow.

OTHELLO   Amen to that, sweet Powers!
I cannot speak enough of this content;
It stops me here; it is too much of joy.
   They kiss
And this, and this the greatest discords be
That e'er our hearts shall make.

IAGO (*aside*)   O, you are well tuned now!
But I'll set down the pegs that make this music,
As honest as I am.

OTHELLO   Come, let's to the castle.
News, friends; our wars are done; the Turks are drowned.
How does my old acquaintance of this isle?
Honey, you shall be well desired in Cyprus;
I have found great love amongst them. O my sweet,
I prattle out of fashion and I dote
In mine own comforts. I prithee, good Iago,
Go to the bay and disembark my coffers;
Bring thou the Master to the citadel;
He is a good one, and his worthiness
Does challenge much respect. Come, Desdemona,
Once more well met at Cyprus!
               Exeunt all except Iago and Roderigo

IAGO (*to soldiers, who go off*) Do thou meet me presently at the harbour. (*To Roderigo*) Come hither. If thou be'st valiant — as they say base men being in love have then a nobility in their natures more than is native to them — list me. The Lieutenant tonight watches on the court of guard. First, I must tell thee this: Desdemona is directly in love with him.

ACT II SCENE I

186 like to: like.

187 Succeeds: comes next, follows.

188 But that: that ... not.

189 Powers: gods in heaven, 天上的神明。

191 here: i. e. at the throat.

192 And this, and this: 一个吻，再来一个。　**discords**: conflicts, 冲突（指接吻）。

193 well tuned: 琴瑟调和。

194 set down the pegs: loosen the pegs so as to lower the pitch of the string of a musical instrument, 琵琶等的弦轴叫 pegs.

195 As ... am: for all my apparent honesty, 意谓不动声色。**to**: 前面省略 go.

196 done: won.

197 acquaintance: 为集合名词，指 acquaintances.

198 well desired: well received, welcomed.

200 out of fashion: out of customary use.　**dote**: indulge.

201 comforts: happiness, joys.

202 coffers: trunks.

203 Master: captain of the ship.

205 challenge: claim.

208 presently: soon.

210—211 native to: inherent in, 本性具有的。　**list**: listen to.

211 watches: is on watch (night duty).

212 court of guard: guardhouse.

213 directly: plainly, without ambiguity.　**him**: i. e., Cassio.

RODERIGO With him? Why, 'tis not possible!

IAGO Lay thy finger thus, and let thy soul be instructed. Mark me with what violence she first loved the Moor, but for bragging and telling her fantastical lies. And will she love him still for prating? Let not thy discreet heart think it. Her eye must be fed. And what delight shall she have to look on the devil? When the blood is made dull with the act of sport, there should be, again to inflame it and give satiety a fresh appetite, loveliness in favour, sympathy in years, manners and beauties: all which the Moor is defective in. Now for want of these required conveniences, her delicate tenderness will find itself abused, begin to heave the gorge, disrelish and abhor the Moor. Very nature will instruct her in it and compel her to some second choice. Now, sir, this granted — as it is a most pregnant and unforced position — who stands so eminently in the degree of this fortune as Cassio does? — a knave very voluble; no further conscionable than in putting on the mere form of civil and humane seeming for the better compassing of his salt and most hidden loose affection. Why, none; why, none — a slipper and subtle knave, a finder out of occasions; that has an eye can stamp and counterfeit advantages, though true advantage never present itself; a devilish knave! Besides, the knave is handsome, young, and hath all those requisites in him that folly and green minds look after. A pestilent complete knave; and the woman hath found him already.

RODERIGO I cannot believe that in her: she's full of most blessed condition.

IAGO Blessed fig's end! The wine she drinks is made of grapes. If she had been blessed, she would never have loved the Moor. Blessed pudding! Didst thou not see her paddle with the palm of his hand? Didst not mark

215 thus: i. e. on your lips.
216 Mark me: attend to me,听我说。
217 but for: only for.
218 still: always. **discreet**: prudent.
219 think: imagine, believe. **fed**: satisfied.
221 act of sport: sexual activity.
223 favour: face, personal appearance. **sympathy**: agreement, correspondence.
225 conveniences: compatibilities, advantages.
226 abused: ill-treated. **heave the gorge**: be sick, experience nausea. **disrelish**: not like the taste of.
228 this granted: this being admitted as true.
229—230 pregnant: clear, obvious. **unforced**: natural. **position**: supposition.
230 degree: rank, position.
231 voluble: fluent in speech.
232 conscionable: more conscientious.
233 humane seeming: courteous appearance. **compassing**: encompassing, fulfilment.
234 salt: lecherous,淫荡的。 **loose**: licentious.
235—236 slipper (adj.): slippery. **finder out of occasions**: seeker of opportunities. **stamp**: impress,铸造。
236—237 counterfeit: forge,伪造。 **advantages**: opportunities.
240 folly: wantonness. **green**: immature, inexperienced. **complete**: out-and-out.
243 condition: disposition.
244 fig's end: 参见 I. iii 316 注。这里等于说"Blessed 个屁"。
246 pudding: sausage.
247 paddle with: play with, toy with. **Didst**: 后省主语 thou.

that?

RODERIGO Yes, that I did; but that was but courtesy.

IAGO Lechery, by this hand; an index and obscure prologue to the history of lust and foul thoughts. They
met so near with their lips that their breaths embraced
together. Villainous thoughts, Roderigo! When these
mutualities so marshal the way, hard at hand comes the
master and main exercise, th'incorporate conclusion.
Pish! But, sir, be you ruled by me. I have brought you
from Venice. Watch you tonight; for the command,
I'll lay't upon you. Cassio knows you not; I'll not be
far from you. Do you find some occasion to anger Cassio, either by speaking too loud, or tainting his disci-
pline, or from what other course you please, which the
time shall more favourably minister.

RODERIGO Well.

IAGO Sir, he's rash and very sudden in choler, and haply with his truncheon may strike at you; provoke him
that he may, for even out of that will I cause these of
Cyprus to mutiny, whose qualification shall come into
no true taste again but by the displanting of Cassio. So
shall you have a shorter journey to your desires by the
means I shall then have to prefer them, and the impediment most profitably removed, without the which there
were no expectation of our prosperity.

RODERIGO I will do this, if you can bring it to any opportunity.

IAGO I warrant thee. Meet me by and by at the citadel.
I must fetch his necessaries ashore. Farewell.

RODERIGO Adieu. *Exit*

IAGO

That Cassio loves her, I do well believe't;
That she loves him, 'tis apt and of great credit.
The Moor — howbeit that I endure him not —

249　by this hand: I swear by this hand.　**index**: preface, prologue.　**obscure**: hidden.

253　mutualities: exchanges, intimacies.　**marshal**: guide, lead.

254　master and main: chief（一对用 and 连接的双声同义词）。 **incorporate**: incorporated, united into one body, carnal.　**conclusion**: 双关语 1.结论;2. combination, union.

256　Watch you: stand watch tonight ('You' is the subject in this imperative sentence).　**for**: as for.　**command**: order (to stand watch).

257　lay't: impose the order.

258　occasion: chance, reason.

259　tainting: disparaging.

260—261　the time: the future.　**minister**: provide.

262　sudden in choler: impetuous, in anger.

264　haply: perhaps.　**truncheon**: 军棍,警棍。

265　that: so that.　**may**: i. e., may strike at you.　**these**: the people.

266　qualification: condition.

267　true taste: satisfactory state.　**but**: except.　**displanting**: removal.

269—270　prefer: promote.　**them**: i. e., your desires.　**impediment**: obstacle.

270　the which: which.

271　expectation: hope.

274　warrant: assure.　**by and by**: presently.

275　his: i. e., Othello's.

278　apt … credit: likely and very credible.

279　howbeit that: although.

280	Is of a constant, loving, noble nature,
	And, I dare think, he'll prove to Desdemona
	A most dear husband. Now, I do love her too;
	Not out of absolute lust — though peradventure
	I stand accountant for as great a sin —
285	But partly led to diet my revenge
	For that I do suspect the lusty Moor
	Hath leaped into my seat, the thought whereof
	Doth, like a poisonous mineral, gnaw my inwards,
	And nothing can, or shall, content my soul
290	Till I am evened with him, wife for wife;
	Or failing so, yet that I put the Moor
	At least into a jealousy so strong
	That judgement cannot cure. Which thing to do
	If this poor trash of Venice, whom I leash
295	For his quick hunting, stand the putting on,
	I'll have our Michael Cassio on the hip,
	Abuse him to the Moor in the rank garb —
	For I fear Cassio with my night-cap too —
	Make the Moor thank me, love me, and reward me
300	For making him egregiously an ass,
	And practising upon his peace and quiet,
	Even to madness. 'Tis here, but yet confused:
	Knavery's plain face is never seen till used. *Exit*

SCENE II

II. ii   *Enter Herald, with a proclamation*

HERALD It is Othello's pleasure, our noble and valiant General, that upon certain tidings now arrived importing the mere perdition of the Turkish fleet, every man put himself into triumph: some to dance, some to make
5 bonfires, each man to what sport and revels his addiction leads him. For, besides these beneficial news, it is

ACT II SCENE II

283　**peradventure**：perhaps.
284　**accountant**：accountable, liable.
285　**diet**：feed.
286　**For that**：for.
287　**seat**：bed.
288　**poisonous mineral**：poison.　　**inwards**：insides,内脏,肝肠。
290　**am evened**：get even or quits,扳平,报复。
294　**trash**：worthless person, i. e., Roderigo.　　**leash** (v. t.)：用绳拴住猎狗。
295　**For**：to make more eager.　　**stand**：respond, rise to.　　**putting on**：incitement.
296　**on the hip**：at a disadvantage 原意为在摔跤中抓住对方的中心臀部。
297　**Abuse**：slander.　　**rank**：lustful, lascivious.　　**garb**：dress, appearance, semblance.
298　**with ... too**：having an affair with my wife.
300　**egregiously**：notoriously.
301　**practising upon**：plotting against.
303　**used**：(knavery is) practised.

II. ii

3　**mere**：complete.　　**perdition**：destruction.
4　**put himself into**：join.　　**triumph**：public festivity.
6—7　**addiction**：inctination.

the celebration of his nuptial. So much was his pleasure
should be proclaimed. All offices are open, and there is
full liberty of feasting from this present hour of five till
the bell have told eleven. Heaven bless the isle of Cyprus and our noble General Othello! *Exit*

SCENE III

Enter Othello, Desdemona, Cassio, and attendants

OTHELLO
Good Michael, look you to the guard tonight.
Let's teach ourselves that honourable stop,
Not to outsport discretion.

CASSIO
Iago hath direction what to do;
But, notwithstanding, with my personal eye
Will I look to't.

OTHELLO   Iago is most honest.
Michael, good night. Tomorrow with your earliest
Let me have speech with you. (*To Desdemona*) Come, my dear love,
The purchase made, the fruits are to ensue:
That profit's yet to come 'tween me and you.
Good night.

Exeunt Othello, Desdemona, and attendants
Enter Iago

CASSIO Welcome, Iago; we must to the watch.

IAGO Not this hour, Lieutenant; 'tis not yet ten o'th'-clock. Our General cast us thus early for the love of his Desdemona; who let us not therefore blame. He hath not yet made wanton the night with her; and she is sport for Jove.

CASSIO She is a most exquisite lady.

IAGO And, I'll warrant her, full of game.

8 should: 前省略 which.   **All … open**: There are free food and drink for all.   **offices**: kitchens and storerooms.

10 told: counted, struck.

II. iii

1 look to: attend to, take care of.

2 stop: restraint.

3 outsport discretion: let the fun go beyond the bounds of.

5 notwithstanding: nevertheless.

7 with your earliest: at your earliest convenience.

10 profit: benefit (of our marriage).

12 must to: must go to.

14 cast: dismissed.

15 who: whom, 指 Othello.

16 made wanton … with her: made love to her.

17 sport: good object of love play.

19 warrant: guarantee for.   **game**: amorous play.

20 CASSIO Indeed, she is a most fresh and delicate creature.
IAGO What an eye she has! Methinks it sounds a parley to provocation.
CASSIO An inviting eye, and yet methinks right modest.
IAGO And when she speaks, is it not an alarum to love?
25 CASSIO She is indeed perfection.
IAGO Well, happiness to their sheets! Come, Lieutenant, I have a stoup of wine; and here without are a brace of Cyprus gallants that would fain have a measure to the health of black Othello.
30 CASSIO Not tonight, good Iago. I have very poor and unhappy brains for drinking. I could well wish courtesy would invent some other custom of entertainment.
IAGO O, they are our friends! But one cup; I'll drink for you.
35 CASSIO I have drunk but one cup tonight, and that was craftily qualified too; and behold what innovation it makes here. I am unfortunate in the infirmity and dare not task my weakness with any more.
IAGO What, man! 'Tis a night of revels; the gallants
40 desire it.
CASSIO Where are they?
IAGO Here, at the door: I pray you call them in.
CASSIO I'll do't, but it dislikes me.
IAGO

If I can fasten but one cup upon him,
45 With that which he hath drunk tonight already,
He'll be as full of quarrel and offence
As my young mistress' dog. Now my sick fool Roderigo,
Whom love hath turned almost the wrong side out,
To Desdemona hath tonight caroused
50 Potations pottle-deep; and he's to watch.
Three else of Cyprus, noble swelling spirits —
That hold their honours in a wary distance,

ACT II SCENE III

21　sounds a parley：吹某种号音表示愿谈判停战的条件，这里借用中世纪的军事用语，意谓发出接触的信号，目的不是 to armistice，却是 to provocation.

23　right：very.

24　alarum：call to arms 也是号角声。

26　happiness to：I wish happiness to.

27　stoup：two-quart tankard.　　**without**：outside.

28　brace：pair.　　**gallants**：men of fashion and pleasure.　　**fain**：gladly.　　**have a measure**：drink a quantity of wine (as a toast).

31　unhappy：wretched.　　**courtesy**：etiquette.

33　But：only. 下 35、44 行同。

36　craftily qualified：cunningly diluted.　　**innovation**：disturbance, commotion.

37　here：i. e., in his head.　　**infirmity**：(said ironically) weakness, aptness to get drunk.

38　task：put a strain upon, put … to the proof.

43　dislikes：无人称动词，相当于 displeases.

44　fasten：face … to accept.

47　sick：lovesick.

48　turned … out：turned inside out.

49—50　caroused … pottle-deep：drunk draughts to the bottom of pottle (tankard).

51　else：others.　　**swelling**：proud.　　**spirits**：men.

52　hold … in a wary distance：protect … with a distance cautiously, 警惕地保护住荣誉不让敌人靠近(比剑用语)。

The very elements of this warlike isle —
Have I tonight flustered with flowing cups,
55 And they watch too. Now 'mongst this flock of drunkards,
Am I to put our Cassio in some action
That may offend the isle. But here they come;
If consequence do but approve my dream,
My boat sails freely both with wind and stream.

Enter Cassio with Montano and Gentlemen, and servants with wine

60 CASSIO 'Fore God, they have given me a rouse already.

MONTANO Good faith, a little one; not past a pint, as I am a soldier.

IAGO Some wine, ho!

(*sings*) And let me the canakin clink, clink;
65   And let me the canakin clink;
        A soldier's a man
        O, man's life's but a span;
      Why, then, let a soldier drink.

Some wine, boys.

70 CASSIO 'Fore God, an excellent song.

IAGO I learned it in England, where indeed they are most potent in potting. Your Dane, your German, and your swag-bellied Hollander — drink, ho! — are nothing to your English.

75 CASSIO Is your Englishman so expert in his drinking?

IAGO Why, he drinks you with facility your Dane dead drunk; he sweats not to overthrow your Almaine; he gives your Hollander a vomit, ere the next pottle can be filled.

80 CASSIO To the health of our General!

MONTANO I am for it, Lieutenant; and I'll do you justice.

IAGO O, sweet England!

53 very elements: true representatives.

54 flustered: made hot and excited.

56 put ... in: incite to.

58 consequence: consequent events.　**approve**: prove to be true.

60 'Fore: before.　**rouse**: bumper, draught of liquor.

61—62 as ... soldier：以军人的荣誉担保。

65 canakin: cannikin, small can.

67 span：一拃宽，拇指和小指两端间距离，喻短。

72 potent in potting: strong (capacious) in drinking，注意头韵。

73—74 swag-bellied: big-and-loose-bellied.　**are nothing to**: can't compare with.　**your**：这里和下面许多是庸俗的口语，用法带有贬义。

76 drinks you：这里 you 是 ethical dative，仅起加强语气作用。

77 sweats not: has no need to labour excessively.　**Almaine**: German.

78 gives ... vomit: drinks as much as will make a Dutchman throw up.　**ere**: before.

81—82 do you justice: drink as much as you.

   (*sings*) King Stephen was and-a worthy peer,
     His breeches cost him but a crown;
   He held them sixpence all too dear;
   With that he called the tailor lown.
   He was a wight of high renown.
     And thou art but of low degree;
   'Tis pride that pulls the country down;
   Then take thine auld cloak about thee.
 Some wine, ho!

CASSIO 'Fore God, this is a more exquisite song than the other.

IAGO Will you hear't again?

CASSIO No, for I hold him to be unworthy of his place that does those things. Well, God's above all; and there be souls must be saved, and there be souls must not be saved.

IAGO It's true, good Lieutenant.

CASSIO For mine own part — no offence to the General, nor any man of quality — I hope to be saved.

IAGO And so do I too, Lieutenant.

CASSIO Ay, but, by your leave, not before me. The Lieutenant is to be saved before the Ancient. Let's have no more of this; let's to our affairs. God forgive us our sins. Gentlemen, let's look to our business. Do not think, gentlemen, I am drunk; this is my Ancient, this is my right hand, and this is my left. I am not drunk now; I can stand well enough and I speak well enough.

GENTLEMAN Excellent well.

CASSIO Why, very well; you must not think then that I am drunk.   *Exit*

MONTANO To th'platform, masters; come, let's set the watch.

IAGO
 You see this fellow that is gone before;

84 King Stephen：这一诗节取自伊丽莎白时代的民歌"Take thy old cloak about thee"(披上你的旧斗篷)，见 Thomas Percy：Reliques of Ancient English Poetry (1765).　　**and-a**：a 此处 and 为垫词，无意义。

85　crown：英国以前值 5 先令的硬币。

86　sixpence … dear：too dear by sixpence, 6 便士合半先令。

87　lown：rascal.

88　wight：person.

90　pride：i. e. extravagance in dress.

91　auld：old.

98　be souls must：are souls that must.

102　quality：rank.

104　leave：permission.

106　let's to：let us look to.

111　Excellent (adv.)：exccedingly.

114—115　platform：the level place on the ramparts where the cannonts were mounted.　　**set the watch**：mount the guard.

He is a soldier, fit to stand by Caesar
And give direction; and do but see his vice:
'Tis to his virtue a just equinox,
120 The one as long as th'other. 'Tis pity of him.
I fear the trust Othello puts in him,
On some odd time of his infirmity,
Will shake this island.

MONTANO   But is he often thus?

IAGO
'Tis evermore the prologue to his sleep:
125 He'll watch the horologe a double set,
If drink rock not his cradle.

MONTANO   It were well
The General were put in mind of it:
Perhaps he sees it not, or his good nature
Prizes the virtue that appears in Cassio
130 And looks not on his evils. Is not this true?

Enter Roderigo

IAGO
(*aside*) How now, Roderigo!
I pray you after the Lieutenant go!   *Exit Roderigo*

MONTANO
And 'tis great pity that the noble Moor
Should hazard such a place as his own second
135 With one of an ingraft infirmity.
It were an honest action to say
So to the Moor.

IAGO   Not I, for this fair island!
I do love Cassio well and would do much
To cure him of this evil.
(*Cry within*) 'Help! Help!'
140   But hark, what noise?

Enter Cassio, pursuing Roderigo

CASSIO Zounds, you rogue, you rascal!

117 Caesar：['si:zə，拉丁文读 'kaisə]裘力斯·凯撒（101—44 B. C.）是古罗马战功显赫的大将，征服了欧亚非三洲许多地方。

119 'Tis：i. e., his vice is. **just equinox** ['i:kwinɔks]：昼夜平分时，春（秋）分；exact equal.

122 On some odd time：at a certain time.

123 Will shake 的主语为 trust.

124 evermore：ever, always.

125 watch ... set：remain awake twice around the clock.

126 rock not his cradle：does not put him to sleep. **were**：would be.

127 句首省略 if. **put in mind**：made aware.

131 How now：What is the meaning of this.

134 hazard：risk. **second**：assistant, lieutenant.

135 ingraft (p. p.)：t 后面的 ed 省略，engrafted, inveterate.

136 were：would be. **action**：读三音节[æktiːən].

137 for：for the sake of.

140 hark：listen.

141 Zounds：by God's wounds(赌咒语)。

MONTANO What's the matter, Lieutenant?

CASSIO A knave teach me my duty? I'll beat the knave into a twiggen-bottle.

RODERIGO Beat me?

CASSIO Dost thou prate, rogue?

He strikes Roderigo

MONTANO Nay, good Lieutenant; I pray you, sir, hold your hand.

CASSIO Let me go, sir, or I'll knock you o'er the mazzard.

MONTANO Come, come, you're drunk.

CASSIO Drunk!

IAGO (*to Roderigo*) Away, I say; go out and cry a mutiny.

Exit Roderigo

Nay, good Lieutenant. God's will, gentleman!
Help, ho! Lieutenant! Sir! Montano! Sir!
Help, masters. Here's a goodly watch indeed.
   Bell rings
Who's that which rings the bell? Diablo, ho!
The town will rise. God's will, Lieutenant, hold!
You will be shamed for ever!
   Enter Othello and attendants

OTHELLO
   What is the matter here?

MONTANO   Zounds, I bleed still.
   I am hurt to th'death.

OTHELLO   Hold for your lives!

IAGO
Hold, ho, Lieutenant, sir, Montano, gentlemen!
Have you forgot all sense of place and duty?
Hold! The General speaks to you: hold, for shame!

OTHELLO
Why, how now, ho! From whence ariseth this?

143 knave: servant, low person. **twiggen-bottle**: wicker-covered bottle, 打得全是鞭痕, 像藤条 twig 的编织物似的。

148 mazzard: (俚语)mazad, head (原意野樱桃)。

151 mutiny: disorder.

152 God's will: by God's will(赌咒语)。

154 masters: gentlemen. **goodly**: fine.

155 Diablo: the devil.

159 Hold ... lives: 要活命的快住手。

161 forgot: forgotten.

163 how now: 见 131 注。

Are we turned Turks and to ourselves do that
165 Which heaven hath forbid the Ottomites?
For Christian shame, put by this barbarous brawl.
He that stirs next to carve for his own rage
Holds his soul light: he dies upon his motion.
Silence that dreadful bell: it frights the isle
170 From her propriety. What is the matter, masters?
Honest Iago, that looks dead with grieving,
Speak, who began this? On thy love I charge thee.
IAGO

I do not know. Friends all but now, even now,
In quarter and in terms like bride and groom
175 Devesting them for bed: and then but now —
As if some planet had unwitted men —
Swords out, and tilting one at others' breasts
In opposition bloody. I cannot speak
Any beginning to this peevish odds;
180 And would in action glorious I had lost
Those legs that brought me to a part of it.
OTHELLO

How comes it, Michael, you are thus forgot?
CASSIO

I pray you pardon me: I cannot speak.
OTHELLO

Worthy Montano, you were wont to be civil:
185 The gravity and stillness of your youth
The world hath noted; and your name is great
In mouths of wisest censure. What's the matter
That you unlace your reputation thus
And spend your rich opinion for the name
190 Of a night-brawler? Give me answer to it.
MONTANO

Worthy Othello, I am hurt to danger.
Your officer, Iago, can inform you,

ACT II SCENE III

164 turned: changed into.

165 forbid: forbidden.

166 put by: desist from, give up.   **brawl**: noisy quarrel.

167 carve for: indulge.

168 Holds ... light: values little.   **upon his motion**: at his first movement.

169 Silence (v. t.): put to silence.   **frights**: frightens.

170 propriety: proper state or condition.

171 dead: deadly pale.

172 charge thee: order you to speak.

174 In quarter: keep good quarter, in good order.   **in terms**: on good terms.

175 Devesting: divesting, undressing.   **them**: themselves.

176 planet had unwitted: star had deprived ... of their wits. 在伊丽莎白时代，人们相信人的行为受星宿的影响。

177 tilting: thrusting.   **tilting one**: one tilting.

178 speak: explain.

179 peevish odds: silly quarrel.

180 would: wish.

182 you are thus forgot: you have forgotten yourself thus.

184 won to: accustomed to.   **civil**: well-behaved.

185 gravity: seriousness, 严肃。   **stillness**: staid behaviour.

187 censure: judgement.

188 unlace: undo, give up.

189 spend ... opinion: lose your good reputation.

191 hurt to danger: seriously injured.

While I spare speech, which something now offends me,
Of all that I do know; nor know I aught
195 By me that's said or done amiss this night
Unless self-charity be sometimes a vice,
And to defend ourselves it be a sin
When violence assails us.

OTHELLO   Now, by heaven,
My blood begins my safer guides to rule,
200 And passion, having my best judgement collied,
Assays to lead the way. Zounds, if I stir,
Or do but lift this arm, the best of you
Shall sink in my rebuke. Give me to know
How this foul rout began, who set it on;
205 And he that is approved in this offence,
Though he had twinned with me, both at a birth,
Shall lose me. What! In a town of war
Yet wild, the people's hearts brimful of fear,
To manage private and domestic quarrel
210 In night, and on the court and guard of safety,
'Tis monstrous. Iago, who began't?

MONTANO

If partially affined or leagued in office,
Thou dost deliver more or less than truth,
Thou art no soldier.

IAGO   Touch me not so near.
215 I had rather have this tongue cut from my mouth
Than it should do offence to Michael Cassio.
Yet, I persuade myself, to speak the truth
Shall nothing wrong him. This it is, General.
Montano and myself being in speech,
220 There comes a fellow, crying out for help,
And Cassio following with determined sword
To execute upon him. Sir, this gentleman
Steps in to Cassio and entreats his pause;

ACT II SCENE III

193　spare speech: refrain to speak.　**something** (adv.): somewhat.　**offends**: pains.

194　Of ... know: 为定语,修饰上行 speech.　**aught**: anything.

195　amiss: wrong.

196　self-charity: love for oneself, self-defense.

197　And it is a sin to defend ourselves, 倒序时 it 似多余。

199　blood: passion of anger.　**guides**: i. e., reason.

200　collied: darkened 原意为被煤粉抹黑。

201　Assays: tries.　**stir**: act.

203　rebuke: reprimand.　**Give ... know**: let me know.

204　rout: riot, uproar.　**set it on**: incite it.

205　approved in: found guilty of.

206　had twinned with me: were twins with me.

207　town of war: town at war.

208　wild: disordered, agitated.　**brimful of**: full of.

209　manage: carry on.

210　In night: in the night, at night.　**on ... safety**: at the guardhouse and on watch.　**safety**: safeguard.

212　partially ... office: made partial by close relationship or being fellow officers.

213　deliver: report.

214　Touch: affect, strike.　**near**: closely.

218　nothing (adv.): not.　**wrong** (v.): be unjust to, 冤屈。 **This it is**: it is like this.

219　in speech: in conversation.

222　execute upon: give effect to or wreak a passion (his anger) upon.　**this gentleman**: 指 Montano.

223　entreats his pause: begs him to stop.

Myself the crying fellow did pursue
225 Lest by his clamour — as it so fell out —
The town might fall in fright. He, swift of foot,
Outran my purpose and I returned the rather
For that I heard the clink and fall of swords
And Cassio high in oath, which till tonight
230 I ne'er might say before. When I came back —
For this was brief — I found them close together
At blow and thrust, even as again they were
When you yourself did part them.
More of this matter can I not report:
235 But men are men; the best sometimes forget.
Though Cassio did some little wrong to him,
As men in rage strike those that with them best,
Yet surely Cassio, I believe, received
From him that fled some strange indignity
240 Which patience could not pass.

OTHELLO   I know, Iago,
Thy honesty and love doth mince this matter,
Making it light to Cassio. Cassio, I love thee,
But nevermore be officer of mine.

Enter Desdemona, attended

Look, if my gentle love be not raised up.
245 I'll make thee an example.

DESDEMONA   What is the matter, dear?

OTHELLO

All's well now, sweeting: come away to bed.
Sir, for your hurts myself will be your surgeon.

Montano is led off

Iago, look with care about the town
And silence those whom this vile brawl distracted.
250 Come, Desdemona, 'tis the soldiers' life
To have their balmy slumbers waked with strife.

Exeunt all but Iago and Cassio

ACT II SCENE III

225 **fell out**: happened.
226 **fall in**: pass into a state of.
227 **rather**: sooner.
228 **For that**: for.
229 **high**: loud.
235 **forget**: forget themselves.
239 **indignity**: insult.
240 **pass**: pass over.
241 **mince**: extenuate, make light of.
244 **raised**: roused.
245 **make ... example**: make an example of you, 拿你做一个例子（以警戒其他人）。
246 **sweeting**: sweatheart.
247 **be your surgeon**: i. e. , see that you receive medical attention.
249 **distracted**: bewildered, perplexed.
251 **balmy slumbers**: soothing sleep. **waked**: disturbed.

IAGO What, are you hurt, Lieutenant?

CASSIO Ay, past all surgery.

IAGO Marry, God forbid!

255 CASSIO Reputation, reputation, reputation! O, I have lost my reputation! I have lost the immortal part of myself, and what remains is bestial. My reputation, Iago, my reputation!

IAGO As I am an honest man I thought you had received
260 some bodily wound; there is more of sense in that than in reputation. Reputation is an idle and most false imposition; oft got without merit and lost without deserving. You have lost no reputation at all, unless you repute yourself such a loser. What, man! There are ways
265 to recover the General again. You are but now cast in his mood — a punishment more in policy than in malice — even so as one would beat his offenceless dog to affright an imperious lion. Sue to him again, and he's yours.

270 CASSIO I will rather sue to be despised than to deceive so good a commander with so slight, so drunken, and so indiscreet an officer. Drunk! And speak parrot! And squabble! Swagger! Swear! And discourse fustian with one's own shadow! O, thou invisible spirit of wine, if
275 thou hast no name to be known by, let us call thee devil.

IAGO What was he that you followed with your sword? What had he done to you?

CASSIO I know not.

IAGO Is't possible?

280 CASSIO I remember a mass of things, but nothing distinctly; a quarrel, but nothing wherefore. O God, that men should put an enemy in their mouths to steal away their brains! That we should with joy, pleasance, revel and applause transform ourselves into beasts!

ACT II SCENE III

257　bestial ['bestjəl]: of the beast, mortal.

261　idle: worthless, useless.

262　imposition: a thing imposed from outside, attachment.

263　deserving: good reason.

264　repute: think of, reckon.

265　recover: regain favour or friendship with.　**cast**: dismissed.

266　in his mood: in a moment of his anger.　**in policy**: as a measure of public policy.

267—268　beat … lion: (英谚)Beat the dog before the lion, 类似中国谚语"杀鸡给猴看"。

268　affright: frighten.　**imperious**: kingly, majestic.　**Sue**: petition.

271　slight: worthless.

272　speak parrot: speak nonsense.

273—274　squabble: quarrel.　**discourse**: talk.　**fustian**: rubbish.

281　nothing wherefore: not why.

283　pleasance: pleasure.

285 IAGO Why, but you are now well enough! How came you thus recovered?

CASSIO It hath pleased the devil drunkenness to give place to the devil wrath; one unperfectness shows me another, to make me frankly despise myself.

290 IAGO Come, you are too severe a moraller. As the time, the place and the condition of this country stands, I could heartily wish this had not so befallen; but since it is as it is, mend it for your own good.

CASSIO I will ask him for my place again; he shall tell me
295 I am a drunkard. Had I as many mouths as Hydra, such an answer would stop them all. To be now a sensible man, by and by a fool, and presently a beast! O, strange! Every inordinate cup is unblessed and the ingredience is a devil.

300 IAGO Come, come; good wine is a good familiar creature if it be well used; exclaim no more against it. And, good Lieutenant, I think you think I love you.

CASSIO I have well approved it, sir. I drunk!

IAGO You or any man living may be drunk at a time,
305 man. I'll tell you what you shall do. Our General's wife is now the General. I may say so in this respect, for that he hath devoted and given up himself to the contemplation, mark, and denotement of her parts and graces. Confess yourself freely to her; importune her
310 help to put you in your place again. She is of so free, so kind, so apt, so blessed a disposition, that she holds it a vice in her goodness not to do more than she is requested. This broken joint between you and her husband, entreat her to splinter; and my fortunes against
315 any lay worth naming, this crack of your love shall grow stronger than it was before.

CASSIO You advise me well.

IAGO I protest in the sincerity of love and honest kindness.

288 unperfectness: imperfection.

289 frankly: unreservedly.

290 moraller: moralizer.

295 Hydra: 希腊神话中的多头水蛇。

298—299 inordinate: excessive. **ingredience**: contents, ingredients.

300 familiar: friendly.

302 think: believe.

303 approved: proved. **I drunk**: 我竟然醉了！（为主语直接加表语的一种感叹句）

304 at a time: at one time, for once.

308 denotement: careful observation.

309 importune: urgently and persistently asked for.

310 free: generous.

311 apt: easily impressed, impressionable, 易受感动的。

314 splinter(v.): bind with splints, 用夹板扎好（断裂的关节）（为外科医术比喻）。

315 lay: bet(我以我的命运和任何赌注打赌)。

318 protest: vow.

320   CASSIO I think it freely; and betimes in the morning I
will beseech the virtuous Desdemona to undertake for
me. I am desperate of my fortunes if they check me
here.

      IAGO You are in the right. Good night, Lieutenant, I
must to the watch.

325   CASSIO Good night, honest Iago.   *Exit*

      IAGO

    And what's he then that says I play the villain,
    When this advice is free I give, and honest,
    Probal to thinking, and indeed the course
    To win the Moor again? For 'tis most easy
330   Th'inclining Desdemona to subdue
    In any honest suit. She's framed as fruitful
    As the free elements; and then for her
    To win the Moor, were't to renounce his baptism,
    All seals and symbols of redeemèd sin,
335   His soul is so enfettered to her love,
    That she may make, unmake, do what she list,
    Even as her appetite shall play the god
    With his weak function. How am I then a villain
    To counsel Cassio to this parallel course
340   Directly to his good? Divinity of hell!
    When devils will the blackest sins put on,
    They do suggest at first with heavenly shows
    As I do now. For whiles this honest fool
    Plies Desdemona to repair his fortunes
345   And she for him pleads strongly to the Moor,
    I'll pour this pestilence into his ear:
    That she repeals him for her body's lust,
    And by how much she strives to do him good,
    She shall undo her credit with the Moor.
350   So will I turn her virtue into pitch,
    And out of her own goodness make the net

320 **think**: believe.　**freely**: unreservedly.　**betimes**: early.

321—322　**undertake for me**: take my part,替我说话。

322　**I … here**: I despair of my future if my career is stopped short here.

327　**free**: ①free from guile, innocent; ②free of charge.

328　**Probal**: probable.

330　**inclining**: compliant, sympathetic.　**subdue**: persuade.

331　**suit**: request, entreaty.　**framed**: made.　**fruitful**: generous.

332　**free elements**: elements of nature; earth, air, fire and water.

333　**were't**: even if it were.　**baptism**: 基督教的洗礼。

334　**seals**: tokens, signs.　**redeemèd sin**: 按照基督教义,人皆有罪,靠耶稣救赎。

336　**list** (v. i.): like.

337　**appetite**: desire for sexual activity.

338　**function**: operation of intellectual or moral powers.

339　**parallel** (adj.): corresponding.

340　**Divinity of hell**: sacredness of black sin! 佛面蛇心的鬼魅(系伊阿古形容自己的词语)。

341　**put on**: instigate.

342　**suggest**: seduce.

344　**Plies**: approach repeatedly with demand.

347　**repeals him**: seeks his reall,要求给他复职。

350　**pitch**: 沥青(被认为是最黑最脏的东西)。

That shall enmesh them all.
Enter Roderigo

How now, Roderigo?

RODERIGO I do follow here in the chase, not like a hound
that hunts, but one that fills up the cry. My money is
almost spent; I have been tonight exceedingly well
cudgelled; and I think the issue will be, I shall have so
much experience for my pains; and so, with no money
at all, and a little more wit, return again to Venice.

IAGO

How poor are they that have not patience!
What wound did ever heal but by degrees?
Thou know'st we work by wit, and not by witchcraft,
And wit depends on dilatory time.
Does't not go well? Cassio hath beaten thee,
And thou by that small hurt hath cashiered Cassio.
Though other things grow fair against the sun,
Yet fruits that blossom first will first be ripe.
Content thyself awhile. By th'mass, 'tis morning;
Pleasure and action make the hours seem short.
Retire thee; go where thou art billeted.
Away, I say, thou shalt know more hereafter;
Nay, get thee gone. *Exit Roderigo*
Two things are to be done.
My wife must move for Cassio to her mistress;
I'll set her on.
Myself the while to draw the Moor apart,
And bring him jump when he may Cassio find
Soliciting his wife. Ay, that's the way.
Dull not device by coldness and delay. *Exit*

352 **enmesh**: entangle.

354 **fills up**: 凑数。 **cry**: pack,猎狗群。

356 **issue**: result.

357 **experience**: lesson. **pains**: painstaking efforts,费的劲。

358 **wit**: wisdom.

360 **but**: except.

362 **dilatory**: given to delay.

364 **cashiered**: fired(开除), made possible the discharge of Cassio.

365 **against the sun**: in face of the sun, with sunshine.

367 **by th'mass**: 赌咒语(mass 弥撒)。

369 **billeted**: lodged, assigned living quarters.

372 **move for**: petition for,请求。 **her mistress**: 指 Desdemona.

373 **set on**: instigate, incite,唆使。

375 **jump** (adv.): exactly, just.

377 **Dull not**: do not make ineffective. **device**: plot. **coldness**: lack of zeal.

ACT III

SCENE I

III.i *Enter Cassio and Musicians*

CASSIO

Masters, play here — I will content your pains —
Something that's brief; and bid 'Good morrow, General'.
  They play
  Enter Clown

CLOWN Why, masters, have your instruments been in Naples, that they speak i'th'nose thus?

5 FIRST MUSICIAN How, sir, how?

CLOWN Are these, I pray you, wind instruments?

FIRST MUSICIAN Ay, marry are they, sir.

CLOWN O, thereby hangs a tail.

FIRST MUSICIAN Whereby hangs a tale, sir?

10 CLOWN Marry, sir, by many a wind instrument that I know. But, masters, here's money for you: and the General so likes your music that he desires you, for love's sake, to make no more noise with it.

FIRST MUSICIAN Well, sir, we will not.

15 CLOWN If you have any music that may not be heard, to't again. But, as they say, to hear music the General does not greatly care.

FIRST MUSICIAN We have none such, sir.

CLOWN Then put up your pipes in your bag, for I'll
20 away. Go, vanish into air, away.   *Exeunt Musicians*

CASSIO Dost thou hear, mine honest friend?

CLOWN No, I hear not your honest friend: I hear you.

III. i

1　content … pains：reward your labour.

2　Something：some melody.　　**Good morrow**：good morning.

4　Naples：该地人说意大利语带鼻音,其原因是他们多患梅毒。

6　wind instrument：管乐器。

7　marry are they：well, they are (marry 为 By Mary 的缩语,温和的赌咒语)。

8　thereby：在那旁边。　　**hangs a tail**：挂着一条尾巴(影射男性生殖器)。

9　Whereby … tale：在那里有个典故(故事),因 tail 和 tale 发音相同而误解或作文字游戏。

15　may：can.

16　to't：go to it, play it.

20　away：go away.

CASSIO Prithee keep up thy quillets — there's a poor
piece of gold for thee. If the gentlewoman that attends
the General's wife be stirring, tell her there's one
Cassio entreats her a little favour of speech. Wilt thou
do this?

CLOWN She is stirring, sir. If she will stir hither, I shall
seem to notify unto her.

CASSIO Do, good my friend.   *Exit Clown*
    Enter Iago

In happy time, Iago.

IAGO   You have not been abed then?

CASSIO

Why, no; the day had broke before we parted.
I have made bold, Iago,
To send in to your wife. My suit to her
Is that she will to virtuous Desdemona
Procure me some access.

IAGO   I'll send her to you presently;
And I'll devise a mean to draw the Moor
Out of the way, that your converse and business
May be more free.

CASSIO   I humbly thank you for't.

                                            Exit Iago

I never knew a Florentine more kind and honest.
    Enter Emilia

EMILIA

Good morrow, good Lieutenant; I am sorry
For your displeasure; but all will sure be well.
The General and his wife are talking of it,
And she speaks for you stoutly. The Moor replies
That he you hurt is of great fame in Cyprus,
And great affinity; and that in wholesome wisdom
He might not but refuse you; but he protests he loves
    you

23 keep up: put away.　**quillets**: quips, plays on words.

25 stirring: up and about.

26 entreats: i. e., 其前省略 who.　**a little favour of speech**: the favour of a brief talk.

28 notify: give information.

30 In happy time: i. e., well met.

31 broke: broken.

33 send in: i. e., send a message in.　**suit**: appeal.

35 Procure me some access: get me a way of approach (下接上行的 to).　**presently**: immediately.

36 mean: means.

37 that: so that.　**converse** ['kɔnvəs]: talk, conversation.

38 free: i. e., from interference.

39 Florentine: native of Florence, 以善良正直闻名。伊阿古虽是威尼斯人，凯西奥认为他比任何一个佛罗伦萨同乡还要好。

41 displeasure: fall from favour.　**sure**: surely.

43 stoutly: boldly, resolutely.

44 he: the person 后面省略 whom.

45 affinity: relation or connexion of any kind, 此处接上文为 of great affinity, 即 have great people for his relations or friends.　**wholesome**: reasonable, sensible.

46 might: could.　**refuse**: reject, dismiss.　**protests**: declare.

　　　　And needs no other suitor but his likings
　　　　To take the safest occasion by the front
　　　　To bring you in again.
　　CASSIO　　　　　　　　　Yet I beseech you,
50　　If you think fit, or that it may be done,
　　　　Give me advantage of some brief discourse
　　　　With Desdemona alone.
　　EMILIA　　　　　　　　　Pray you, come in:
　　　　I will bestow you where you shall have time
　　　　To speak your bosom freely.
　　CASSIO　　　　　　　　　I am much bound to you.
　　　　　　　　　　　　　　　　　　　　　　Exeunt

SCENE II

III. ii　　*Enter Othello, Iago, and Gentlemen*

　　OTHELLO
　　　　These letters give, Iago, to the pilot,
　　　　And by him do my duties to the senate.
　　　　That done, I will be walking on the works:
　　　　Repair there to me.
　　IAGO　　　　　　　　Well, my good lord, I'll do't. *Exit*
　　OTHELLO
5　　This fortification, gentlemen, shall we see't?
　　GANTLEMEN
　　　　We'll wait upon your lordship.　　　　　*Exeunt*

SCENE III

III. iii　　*Enter Desdemona, Cassio, and Emilia*

　　DESDEMONA
　　　　Be thou assured, good Cassio, I will do
　　　　All my abilities in thy behalf.
　　EMILIA

ACT III SCENE II—III

   47   **likings**：affection,对你的喜爱(这里被拟人化为一个 suitor)。

   48   **take**：seize.   **safest**：soundest, best.   **front**：forehead, forelock,马的额毛。(英谚)take time by the forelock,喻抓住机会。

   53   **bestow**(v. t.)：place, put.

   54   **bosom**：intimate thoughts.   **bound**：obliged.

III. ii

   2   **do … duties**：convey my respects.

   3   **works**：breast works, fortification,城堡上的工事。

   4   **Repair**：come.

   6   **wait upon**：attend.

III. iii

   2   **in thy behalf**：on your behalf.

　　　　　Good madam, do; I warrant it grieves my husband
　　　　　As if the case were his.
DESDEMONA

5　　　　O, that's an honest fellow! Do not doubt, Cassio,
　　　　　But I will have my lord and you again
　　　　　As friendly as you were.
CASSIO　　　　　　　　　　Bounteous madam,
　　　　　Whatever shall become of Michael Cassio,
　　　　　He's never anything but your true servant.
DESDEMONA

10　　　　I know't; I thank you. You do love my lord;
　　　　　You have known him long, and be you well assured
　　　　　He shall in strangeness stand no farther off
　　　　　Than in a politic distance.
CASSIO　　　　　　　　　　　Ay, but, lady,
　　　　　That policy may either last so long,

15　　　　Or feed upon such nice and waterish diet,
　　　　　Or breed itself so out of circumstance,
　　　　　That I being absent and my place supplied,
　　　　　My General will forget my love and service.
DESDEMONA
　　　　　Do not doubt that. Before Emilia here,

20　　　　I give thee warrant of thy place. Assure thee,
　　　　　If I do vow a friendship, I'll perform it
　　　　　To the last article. My lord shall never rest.
　　　　　I'll watch him tame and talk him out of patience;
　　　　　His bed shall seem a school, his board a shrift;

25　　　　I'll intermingle everything he does
　　　　　With Cassio's suit. Therefore be merry, Cassio,
　　　　　For thy solicitor shall rather die
　　　　　Than give thy cause away.
　　　　　　　　Enter Othello and Iago
EMILIA
　　　　　Madam, here comes my lord.

6 But: that ... not.

7 Bounteous: generous.

12—13 He ... distance: 他的冷淡不过是他官职上的需要,拉开一段距离,不会再走得更远。 **strangeness**: aloofness, alienation. **politic**: required by policy.

15 nice: meagre. **waterish**: thin, poor.

16 out of circumstance: by accident.

17 supplied: being filled (by another).

19 doubt: fear.

20 give ... place: 担保你会官复原职。 **Assure**: 前省略 I.

22 article: detail.

23 watch him tame: keep (a hawk) awake in order to tame it, 借用驯猎鹰用语,使之不得睡眠,直至驯服。

24 board: 饭桌。 **shrift**: confessional,(天主教信徒对神父作)忏悔的所在。

27 solicitor: pleader, 求情者。

28 give ... away: give up.

CASSIO

30 Madam, I'll take my leave.

DESDEMONA

Why, stay and hear me speak.

CASSIO

Madam, not now: I am very ill at ease,
Unfit for mine own purposes.

DESDEMONA

Well, do your discretion.   *Exit Cassio*

IAGO

35 Ha! I like not that.

OTHELLO   What dost thou say?

IAGO

Nothing, my lord; or if — I know not what.

OTHELLO

Was not that Cassio parted from my wife?

IAGO

Cassio, my lord? No, sure, I cannot think it
That he would sneak away so guilty-like,
Seeing you coming.

40 OTHELLO   I do believe 'twas he.

DESDEMONA

How now, my lord?
I have been talking with a suitor here,
A man that languishes in your displeasure.

OTHELLO

Who is't you mean?

DESDEMONA

45 Why, your Lieutenant, Cassio. Good my lord,
If I have any grace or power to move you,
His present reconciliation take.
For if he be not one that truly loves you,
That errs in ignorance, and not in cunning,

50 I have no judgement in an honest face.

33 Unfit ... purposes: in no condition to plead my own case.

34 do your discretion: do as you think fit.

37 Cassio: 后省略 who.

38 think: believe.

46 grace: favour, influence.

47 His ... take: accept his immediate submission aimed at restoring of friendship.

49 in cunning: knowingly, 明知故犯。

I prithee call him back.

OTHELLO

Went he hence now?

DESDEMONA

Yes, faith; so humbled
That he hath left part of his grief with me
To suffer with him. Good love, call him back.

OTHELLO

55 Not now, sweet Desdemon; some other time.

DESDEMONA

But shall't be shortly?

OTHELLO

The sooner, sweet, for you.

DESDEMONA

Shall't be tonight, at supper?

OTHELLO

No, not tonight.

DESDEMONA

Tomorrow dinner then?

OTHELLO

I shall not dine at home.

I meet the captains at the citadel.

DESDEMONA

60 Why, then, tomorrow night, or Tuesday morn,
On Tuesday noon, or night; on Wednesday morn.
I prithee name the time, but let it not
Exceed three days. In faith, he's penitent:
And yet his trespass in our common reason —
65 Save that, they say, the wars must make example
Out of their best — is not almost a fault
T'incur a private check. When shall he come?
Tell me, Othello. I wonder in my soul
What you would ask me that I should deny,
70 Or stand so mammering on? What! Michael Cassio,
That came a-wooing with you? And so many a time —
When I have spoke of you dispraisingly —
Hath ta'en your part, to have so much to do
To bring him in? By'r Lady, I could do much.

52　faith：in faith.
58　dinner：午饭。
59　meet：shall.
64　trespass：offence.　**common reason**：everyday judgment.
65　Save that：were it not that,若不是。　**make example**：请看II. iii 245 注。
66　is：主语为64行的 trespass.　**not almost**：hardly.
67　a private check：even a private reproach.　**shall**：will.
70　mammering：muttering, hesitating.
71　a-wooing：求婚。
72　dispraisingly：pejoratively,贬义地。
73　to have … do：to have so much ado,有这么多麻烦（不定式主语为省略了的 you）。
74　bring him in：reinstate him.　**By'r Lady**：By our Lady,凭圣母马利亚起誓。　**I … much**：If I were you, I could do much.

OTHELLO
Prithee, no more; let him come when he will;
I will deny thee nothing.

DESDEMONA   Why, this is not a boon;
'Tis as I should entreat you wear your gloves
Or feed on nourishing dishes, or keep you warm,
Or sue to you to do a peculiar profit
To your own person. Nay, when I have a suit
Wherein I mean to touch your love indeed
It shall be full of poise and difficult weight,
And fearful to be granted.

OTHELLO   I will deny thee nothing.
Whereon, I do beseech thee, grant me this;
To leave me but a little to myself.

DESDEMONA
Shall I deny you? No; farewell, my lord.

OTHELLO
Farewell, my Desdemona, I'll come to thee straight.

DESDEMONA
Emilia, come. Be as your fancies teach you.
Whate'er you be, I am obedient.

Exeunt Desdemona and Emilia

OTHELLO
Excellent wretch! Perdition catch my soul
But I do love thee! And when I love thee not,
Chaos is come again.

IAGO   My noble lord —

OTHELLO
What dost thou say, Iago?

IAGO   Did Michael Cassio,
When you wooed my lady, know of your love?

OTHELLO
He did, from first to last. Why dost thou ask?

IAGO

ACT III SCENE III

76 **boon**: great favor.
77 **as**: as if.　**wear**: 前省略 to.
79 **peculiar profit**: particular benefit.
81 **touch**: test as with the touchstone (试金石)。
82 **poise**: weight,有分量,很重要。　**difficult**: hard to estimate.
83 **fearful**: expecting with a sense of fear.
84 **Whereon**: in return for which.
85 **but**: only,让我独自待一会儿。
87 **straight**: straightway, directly.
88 **Be ... you**: please yourself.
90 **wretch**: (used as a word of tenderness mixed with pity) 可怜可爱的人儿。　**Perdition**: damnation.
91 **But**: if ... not.
92 **Chaos ... again**: Disorder will have returned.

>   But for a satisfaction of my thought —
>   No further harm.
> OTHELLO   Why of thy thought, Iago?
> IAGO
>   I did not think he had been acquainted with her.
> OTHELLO
>   O yes, and went between us very oft.
> IAGO
> 100   Indeed!
> OTHELLO
>   Indeed? Ay, indeed. Discern'st thou aught in that?
>   Is he not honest?
> IAGO   Honest, my lord?
> OTHELLO   Honest? Ay, honest.
> IAGO
>   My lord, for aught I know.
> OTHELLO   What dost thou think?
> IAGO
>   Think, my lord?
> OTHELLO
> 105   Think, my lord! By heaven, he echoes me,
>   As if there were some monster in his thought
>   Too hideous to be shown. Thou dost mean something.
>   I heard thee say even now, thou lik'st not that,
>   When Cassio left my wife. What didst not like?
> 110   And when I told thee he was of my counsel
>   In my whole course of wooing, thou cried'st 'Indeed!'
>   And didst contract and purse thy brow together,
>   As if thou then hadst shut up in thy brain
>   Some horrible conceit. If thou dost love me,
> 115   Show me thy thought.
> IAGO
>   My lord, you know I love you.
> OTHELLO   I think thou dost;

96　But：only.
101　aught：anything.
103　for … know：as far as I know.
105—107　By … shown：此句为旁白。　**he**：指 Iago.
109　didst：后省略 thou.
110　of my counsel：in my confidence.
112　contract … together：knit your brows，皱眉头。
114　conceit：thought.
116　think：believe.

And for I know thou'rt full of love and honesty,
And weigh'st thy words before thou giv'st them breath,
Therefore these stops of thine affright me more;
120 For such things in a false disloyal knave
Are tricks of custom; but in a man that's just,
They're close dilations, working from the heart,
That passion cannot rule.

IAGO   For Michael Cassio,
I dare be sworn I think that he is honest.

OTHELLO
I think so too.

125 IAGO   Men should be what they seem;
Or those that be not, would they might seem none!

OTHELLO
Certain, men should be what they seem.

IAGO
Why, then, I think Cassio's an honest man.

OTHELLO
Nay, yet there's more in this.
130 I prithee speak to me as to thy thinkings,
As thou dost ruminate, and give thy worst of thoughts
The worst of words.

IAGO   Good my lord, pardon me;
Though I am bound to every act of duty,
I am not bound to that all slaves are free to:
135 Utter my thoughts. Why, say they are vile and false?
As where's that palace whereinto foul things
Sometimes intrude not? Who has a breast so pure,
But some uncleanly apprehensions
Keep leets and law-days, and in session sit
140 With meditations lawful?

OTHELLO
Thou dost conspire against thy friend, Iago,
If thou but think'st him wronged, and mak'st his ear

117 for I know: as far as I know.

118 giv'st them breath: utter them.

119 stops: hesitations, pauses.

121 tricks of custom: customary devices.

122 close: secret, involuntarily revealed.　　**dilations**: ①delays; ②delations, accusations.

123 For: as for.

126 would: I wish.

127 Certain: certainly.

130 prithee: pray you to, beg you to.　　**thy thinkings**: your own thoughts.

131 ruminate: meditate 原意为反刍。

134 bound ... to: bound to reveal what all slaves are permitted to keep to themselves.　　**that**: that which, what.　　**free to**: free with respect to.

135 Why: (语气词)well, 哦。　　**say**: let's say, suppose.　　**they**: 指 my thoughts.

136 As: for example.　　**whereinto**: into which.

138 But: that ... not 后面省略 in it.　　**uncleanly apprehensions**: unwholesome idea.

139 leets: 英国某些庄园设的法庭。　　**law-days**: 法院开庭(日)。**session**: sitting of the court.

140 With meditations lawful: together with innocent ideas (apprehension 和 meditation 都被拟人化了,在人的 breast 里开庭共议)。

141 conspire: plot.　　**thy friend**: 指 Othello 自己。

142—143 but: in any case.　　**and**: i. e., and yet.　　**mak'st ... thoughts**: don't tell him your thoughts.

A stranger to thy thoughts.
IAGO   I do beseech you,
Though I perchance am vicious in my guess —
145 As I confess it is my nature's plague
     To spy into abuses, and of my jealousy
     Shapes faults that are not — that your wisdom then,
     From one that so imperfectly conjects,
     Would take no notice, nor build yourself a trouble
150 Out of his scattering and unsure observance.
     It were not for your quiet nor your good,
     Nor for my manhood, honesty, and wisdom,
     To let you know my thoughts.
OTHELLO   What dost thou mean?
IAGO
     Good name in man and woman, dear my lord,
155 Is the immediate jewel of their souls.
     Who steals my purse, steals trash; 'tis something, nothing;
     'Twas mine, 'tis his, and has been slave to thousands;
     But he that filches from me my good name
     Robs me of that which not enriches him
160 And makes me poor indeed.
OTHELLO   By heaven, I'll know thy thoughts.
IAGO
     You cannot, if my heart were in your hand,
     Nor shall not, whilst 'tis in my custody.
OTHELLO
     Ha!
IAGO O, beware, my lord, of jealousy!
     It is the green-eyed monster, which doth mock
165 The meat it feeds on. That cuckold lives in bliss
     Who certain of his fate loves not his wronger,
     But O, what damnèd minutes tells he o'er,

ACT III SCENE III

144 perchance: by chance, perhaps. **vicious**: malicious.

145 my nature's plague: the curse of my nature, 我生性上的坏毛病。

146 abuses: vices, evils, 邪恶。 **of**: out of. **jealousy**: suspicion.

147 that your wisdom: 上接144行"I do beseech you." **then**: on that account.

148 one: 指Iago自己。

150 scattering: scattered, random. **observance**: observation.

151 were not: would not be. **quiet**: peace of mind.

155 immediate: of direct interest, 切身的。

156 Who: whoever.

158 filches: steals.

159 not enriches him: does not make him rich.

161 if: even if.

164 mock: make sport of, torment.

165—166 meat: heart, victim. **cuckold**: husband of a faithless wife. **That ... wronger**: The cuckold, who, being certain of his fate (ill-fortune), does not love his faithless wife, lives in happiness.

167 tells: counts.

Who dotes yet doubts, suspects yet fondly loves!
OTHELLO
 O misery!
IAGO
170 Poor and content is rich, and rich enough;
But riches fineless is as poor as winter,
To him that ever fears he shall be poor.
Good God, the souls of all my tribe defend
From jealousy!
OTHELLO Why, why is this?
175 Think'st thou I'd make a life of jealousy,
To follow still the changes of the moon
With fresh suspicions? No, to be once in doubt
Is once to be resolved. Exchange me for a goat,
When I shall turn the business of my soul
180 To such exsufflicate and blown surmises,
Matching thy inference. 'Tis not to make me jealous
To say my wife is fair, loves company,
Is free of speech, sings, plays, and dances well;
Where virtue is, these are more virtuous.
185 Nor from mine own weak merits will I draw
The smallest fear or doubt of her revolt,
For she had eyes and chose me. No, Iago,
I'll see before I doubt; when I doubt, prove;
And on the proof, there is no more but this:
190 Away at once with love or jealousy!
IAGO
 I am glad of this; for now I shall have reason
To show the love and duty that I bear you
With franker spirit. Therefore, as I am bound,
Receive it from me. I speak not yet of proof.
195 Look to your wife; observe her well with Cassio.
Wear your eye thus: not jealous, nor secure.
I would not have your free and noble nature,

170 参见(英谚)He who is content in his poverty is wonderfully rich.

171 **fineless**: boundless.

173 **defend**: 正常位置在 the souls 之前，为祈使动词。

175 **I'd**: I would.

176 **still**: always, all the time.

177—178 **to be … resolved**: Whenever I find myself in doubt, I want to settle the matter once and for all.

180 **exsufflicate and blown**: inflated and blown-up.

181 **Matching**: corresponding to. **inference**: allegation.

186 **of**: about. **revolt**: faithlessness.

193 **franker**: more unrestrained. **as I am bound**: i. e., bound to you in duty and love.

195 **Look to**: watch.

196 **Wear … thus**: look like this. **secure**: careless, over-confident.

Out of self-bounty, be abused. Look to't.
I know our country disposition well:
In Venice they do let God see the pranks
They dare not show their husbands; their best conscience
Is not to leave't undone, but keep't unknown.

OTHELLO
Dost thou say so?

IAGO
She did deceive her father, marrying you,
And when she seemed to shake, and fear your looks,
She loved them most.

OTHELLO   And so she did.

IAGO   Why, go to, then!
She that so young could give out such a seeming,
To seel her father's eyes up close as oak —
He thought 'twas witchcraft. — But I am much to blame,
I humbly do beseech you of your pardon
For too much loving you.

OTHELLO   I am bound to thee for ever.

IAGO I see this hath a little dashed your spirits.

OTHELLO
Not a jot, not a jot.

IAGO   In faith, I fear it has.
I hope you will consider what is spoke
Comes from my love. But I do see you're moved.
I am to pray you, not to strain my speech
To grosser issues, nor to larger reach
Than to suspicion.

OTHELLO
I will not.

IAGO   Should you do so, my lord,
My speech should fall into such vile success

198 self-bounty: natural goodness, bounty 原意为恩惠、奖赏。 **abused**: deceived.

199 country disposition: fellow people's temperament.

200 they: i. e. , wives.　　**pranks**: licentious or mischievous tricks.

201 conscience: regard for the dictates of conscience.

202 leave't: leave it (illicit love).

206 go to: come now.

207 give out: present.　　**seeming**: false appearance.

208 seel: blind. 参见 I. iii 266 注。　　**close as oak**: (英谚)as close as oak; 此处等于 close-grained, 橡木纹理细密。

210 beseech you of your pardon: beg your pardon.

211 bound: indebted.

214 spoke: spoken.

215 moved: disturbed, agitated.

216 am to: must.　　**strain**: extend, stretch.

217 grosser issues: greater significances.　　**reach**: scope.

220 should: would.　　**vile success**: evil result.

Which my thoughts aimed not at. Cassio's my worthy
   friend.

My lord, I see you're moved.

OTHELLO   No, not much moved.

I do not think but Desdemona's honest.

IAGO

Long live she so! And long live you to think so!

OTHELLO

225   And yet, how nature erring from itself —

IAGO

Ay, there's the point: as, to be bold with you,
Not to affect many proposèd matches
Of her own clime, complexion, and degree,
Whereto we see in all things nature tends,

230   Foh! One may smell in such a will most rank,
Foul disproportion, thoughts unnatural.
But, pardon me, I do not in position
Distinctly speak of her, though I may fear
Her will, recoiling to her better judgement,

235   May fall to match you with her country forms,
And happily repent.

OTHELLO   Farewell, farewell.

If more thou dost perceive, let me know more.
Set on thy wife to observe. Leave me, Iago.

IAGO

(*going*) My lord, I take my leave.

OTHELLO

240   Why did I marry? This honest creature doubtless
Sees and knows more, much more than he unfolds.

IAGO

(*returning*) My lord, I would I might entreat your
   honour

To scan this thing no farther. Leave it to time.
Although 'tis fit that Cassio have his place,

ACT III SCENE III

223 **but**: that … not. **honest**: chaste.

225 **erring**: straying.

226 **as**: as for example.

227 **affect**: prefer, like. **proposèd matches**: offers of marriage.

228 **clime**: region, country. **complexion**: 肤色。 **degree**: rank, position.

229 **Whereto**: to which. **tends**: inclines.

230 **will**: appetite. **rank**: lustful, foul.

231 **disproportion**: abnormality.

232 **position**: affirmation, assertion.

234 **recoiling**: reverting.

235 **fall**: begin. **match**: compare. **country forms**: her country's norms of handsomeness.

236 **happily**: ①by good hap; ②haply, perhaps. **repent**: repent her marriage to Othello.

238 **Set on**: cause, urge.

243 **scan**: examine.

245   For sure he fills it up with great ability,
        Yet, if you please to hold him off awhile,
        You shall by that perceive him and his means;
        Note if your lady strain his entertainment
        With any strong or vehement importunity —
250   Much will be seen in that. In the meantime,
        Let me be thought too busy in my fears,
        As worthy cause I have to fear I am,
        And hold her free, I do beseech your honour.

OTHELLO

    Fear not my government.

IAGO   I once more take my leave. *Exit*

OTHELLO

255   This fellow's of exceeding honesty,
        And knows all qualities with a learnèd spirit
        Of human dealings. If I do prove her haggard,
        Though that her jesses were my dear heart-strings,
        I'd whistle her off, and let her down the wind
260   To prey at fortune. Haply, for I am black
        And have not those soft parts of conversation
        That chamberers have; or for I am declined
        Into the vale of years — yet that's not much —
        She's gone; I am abused, and my relief
265   Must be to loathe her. O, curse of marriage!
        That we can call these delicate creatures ours
        And not their appetites! I had rather be a toad
        And live upon the vapour of a dungeon
        Than keep a corner in the thing I love
270   For others' uses. Yet 'tis the plague of great ones;
        Prerogatived are they less than the base.
        'Tis destiny unshunnable, like death;
        Even then this forkèd plague is fated to us
        When we do quicken. Desdemona comes;

        Enter Desdemona and Emilia

ACT III SCENE III

247 perceive: see through. **means**: ways.

248 strain: insist on. **entertainment**: employment.

252 As I have worthy cause to fear that I am (too busy in my fear).

253 hold: regard … as. **free**: innocent, free from suspicion.

254 government: self-control.

256—257 qualities: natures, types. **with … dealings**: with wide experience of human relations.

257 haggard: 发情的雌鹰,喻 wild and intractable.

258 Though that: even though. **jesses**: 缠在猎鹰腿上的饰带。

259 down the wind: 让猎鹰顺风飞去,是放走不要她回来。

260 prey at fortune: 捕野食,自谋生计。

261 soft … conversation: social graces.

262 chamberers: courtiers and gallants. **for**: because. **am declined**: have declined.

264 abused: deceived. **relief**: comfort, remedy.

267 toad: 癞蛤蟆。

268 vapour: a visible fluid floating in the atmosphere,浊气,水气。

270 great ones: distinguished men.

271 Prerogatived: privileged. **the base**: those of humble birth.

272 unshunnable: unavoidable.

273 forkèd plague: the cuckold's horns,头上长角,类似汉语中说的戴绿帽子。

274 do quicken: ①become living, are born; ②become alive with maggots.

	If she be false, O, then heaven mocks itself!
275	

275   If she be false, O, then heaven mocks itself!
       I'll not believe't.

DESDEMONA   How now, my dear Othello!
    Your dinner, and the generous islanders
    By you invited, do attend your presence.

OTHELLO
    I am to blame.

DESDEMONA   Why do you speak so faintly?
280   Are you not well?

OTHELLO
    I have a pain upon my forehead here.

DESDEMONA
    Faith, that's with watching; 'twill away again.
    Let me but bind it hard, within this hour
    It will be well.

OTHELLO   Your napkin is too little.
    He puts the handkerchief from him, and she drops it
285   Let it alone. Come, I'll go in with you.

DESDEMONA
    I am very sorry that you are not well.
                        Exeunt Othello and Desdemona

EMILIA
    I am glad I have found this napkin:
    This was her first remembrance from the Moor.
    My wayward husband hath a hundred times
290   Wooed me to steal it; but she so loves the token —
    For he conjured her she should ever keep it —
    That she reserves it evermore about her
    To kiss and talk to. I'll have the work ta'en out,
    And give't Iago.
295   What he will do with it, heaven knows, not I;
    I nothing, but to please his fantasy.
            Enter Iago

IAGO

ACT III SCENE III

277 **generous**: noble.
278 **attend**: wait for.
282 **watching**: lack of sleep, working late into the night.
287 **napkin**: handkerchief.
288 **remembrance**: souvenir keepsake.
289 **wayward**: capricious.
290 **Wooed**: begged.
291 **conjured**: begged with an oath, solemnly instructed.
292 **reserves**: preserves, keep safe. **evermore**: all the time.
293 **work ... out**: pattern copied.
294 **Iago**: 前省略 to.
296 **I nothing**: I will do nothing. **fantasy**: whim.

How now? What do you here alone?

EMILIA

Do not you chide; I have a thing for you.

IAGO

A thing for me? It is a common thing.

EMILIA

300 Ha!

IAGO

To have a foolish wife.

EMILIA

O, is that all? What will you give me now
For that same handkerchief?

IAGO   What handkerchief?

EMILIA

What handkerchief!
305 Why that the Moor first gave to Desdemona;
That which so often you did bid me steal.

IAGO

Hast stol'n it from her?

EMILIA

No, faith, she let it drop by negligence,
And to th'advantage, I, being here, took't up.
310 Look, here it is.

IAGO   A good wench! Give it me.

EMILIA

What will you do with't, that you have been so earnest
To have me filch it?

IAGO (*snatching it*) Why, what is that to you?

EMILIA

If it be not for some purpose of import,
Give't me again. Poor lady, she'll run mad
315 When she shall lack it.

IAGO

Be not acknown on't; I have use for it.

297 What … you: What are you doing? (莎士比亚时期疑问句常不用助动词 do,而直接将句子倒装,并常以现在时代替现在进行时)
299 common: worthless.
301 have: marry.
305 that: that which.
309 to th'advantage: taking the opportunity.
313 import: importance.
315 lack it: find it missing.
316 Be … on't: do not confess knowledge of it.

Go, leave me. *Exit Emilia*

I will in Cassio's lodging lose this napkin,
And let him find it. Trifles light as air
320 Are to the jealous confirmations strong
As proofs of holy writ. This may do something.
The Moor already changes with my poison.
Dangerous conceits are in their natures poisons,
Which at the first are scarce found to distaste,
325 But, with a little act upon the blood,
Burn like the mines of sulphur.

Enter Othello

I did say so.
Look where he comes! Not poppy, nor mandragora,
Nor all the drowsy syrups of the world,
Shall ever medicine thee to that sweet sleep
Which thou owed'st yesterday.

330 OTHELLO Ha, ha, false to me!
IAGO

Why, how now, General! No more of that.

OTHELLO

Avaunt! Be gone! Thou hast set me on the rack.
I swear 'tis better to be much abused,
Than but to know't a little.

IAGO How now, my lord!
OTHELLO

335 What sense had I of her stolen hours of lust?
I saw't not, thought it not, it harmed not me.
I slept the next night well, was free and merry;
I found not Cassio's kisses on her lips.
He that is robbed, not wanting what is stolen,
340 Let him not know't, and he's not robbed at all.

IAGO

I am sorry to hear this.

OTHELLO

ACT III SCENE III

318 **lose**: drop.
320 **the jealous**: jealous persons.　**confirmations**: evidences.
321 **As**: as if.　**holy writ**: the Bible.
323 **conceits**: ideas, imaginings.
324 **scarce**: scarcely.　**distaste** (v.i.): taste unpleasant.
325 **act**: action, operation.
326 **I ... so**: just as I said.
327 **poppy**: opium poppy, 罂粟。　**mandragora**: mandrake, 做麻醉药用的曼德拉草。
328 **drowsy syrups**: sleep-inducing medicines, 催眠药。
329 **medicine** (v.t.): bring by medicinal means.
330 **owed'st**: owned, possessed, had.
332 **Avaunt**: Be off with you.　**rack**: 过去的拉肢刑具。
333 **abused**: deceived.
335 **sense**: perception.
336 **thought** (v.t.): believed, considered.
337 **free**: carefree.
339 **wanting**: missing.

> I had been happy if the general camp,
> Pioners and all, had tasted her sweet body,
> So I had nothing known. O, now, for ever
345 Farewell the tranquil mind! Farewell content!
> Farewell the plumèd troops and the big wars
> That make ambition virtue — O, farewell!
> Farewell the neighing steed, and the shrill trump,
> The spirit-stirring drum, th'ear-piercing fife,
350 The royal banner and all quality,
> Pride, pomp and circumstance of glorious war!
> And, O you mortal engines, whose rude throats
> Th'immortal Jove's dread clamours counterfeit,
> Farewell! Othello's occupation's gone.

IAGO

355 Is't possible, my lord?

OTHELLO

> Villain, be sure thou prove my love a whore;
> Be sure of it: give me the ocular proof,
> Or by the worth of mine eternal soul,
> Thou hadst been better have been born a dog
360 Than answer my waked wrath!

IAGO   Is't come to this?

OTHELLO

> Make me to see't: or, at the least, so prove it
> That the probation bear no hinge nor loop
> To hang a doubt on — or woe upon thy life!

IAGO

> My noble lord —

OTHELLO

365 If thou dost slander her and torture me,
> Never pray more; abandon all remorse;
> On horror's head horrors accumulate;
> Do deeds to make heaven weep, all earth amazed:
> For nothing canst thou to damnation add

342　had been：would have been.

343　Pioners：diggers of mines, lowest rank of soldiers.　**tasted**：enjoyed.

344　So：so long as.

346　plumèd：wearing plumes in the helmet.

347　virtue：virtuous.

348　neighing steed：长嘶的战马。　**trump**：trumpet.

349　fife：军乐队中的横笛。

350　royal：magnificent.　**quality**：military rank.

351　circumstance：ceremonial pageantry, 威武的仪仗队。

352　mortal engines：deadly cannons.

353　Jove's ... clamours：Jupiter's dreadful noises.　**counterfeit**(v. t.)：imitate.

354　occupation's gone：vocation has come to an end.

356　Villain：wretch, used without serious implication of bad qualities, esp. as a term of address.

357　ocular：visual.

360　answer：meet, be punished for.

361　Make ... see：make me see（现代英语中使役动词 make 后作宾补的不定式省 to）。

362　probation：proof.　**hinge ... loop**：both words mean a hook and eye on which something may be hung.

366　remorse：pity, compunction of conscience.

368　amazed：horrified（为 make 的宾补）。

370 Greater than that.
IAGO   O grace! O heaven defend me!
Are you a man? Have you a soul? Or sense?
God bu'y you: take mine office. O wretched fool,
That lov'st to make thine honesty a vice!
O monstrous world! Take note, take note, O world!
375 To be direct and honest is not safe.
I thank you for this profit, and from hence
I'll love no friend, sith love breeds such offence.
OTHELLO
Nay, stay: thou shouldst be honest.
IAGO
I should be wise; for honesty's a fool
And loses that it works for.
380 OTHELLO   By the world,
I think my wife be honest, and think she is not;
I think that thou art just, and think thou art not.
I'll have some proof. Her name that was as fresh
As Dian's visage is now begrimed and black
385 As mine own face. If there be cords or knives,
Poison or fire or suffocating streams,
I'll not endure it. Would I were satisfied!
IAGO
I see, sir, you are eaten up with passion.
I do repent me that I put it to you.
You would be satisfied?
390 OTHELLO   Would! Nay, I will.
IAGO
And may. But how? How satisfied, my lord?
Would you, the supervisor, grossly gape on?
Behold her topped?
OTHELLO   Death and damnation! O!
IAGO
It were a tedious difficulty, I think,

372 God bu'y you: God be with you.   **O wretched fool**: 为 Iago 对自己所用的呼语(vocative)。

373 make thine honesty: carry your honesty so far that it becomes.

374 world: people of the world.

376 profit: profitable lesson.

377 sith: since.   **offence**: harm.

380 that: what.   **By the world**: 赌咒语, 等于 I swear by the world.

381 第一个 think 接 be 假设语气, 是不肯定的; 第二个 think 接 is 是肯定的, 此 think 相当于 believe.

384 Dian: Diana, the Roman goddess of chastity.   **begrimed**: soiled.

386 suffocating streams: streams which drown.

387 Would ... satisfied: How I wish to be convinced beyond doubt.

390 Would ... will: will 比 would 肯定, 语气更坚决。

392 supervisor: spectator.   **grossly**: stupidly.

393 topped: mounted in sexual intercourse.

394 tedious: laborious, irksome.

To bring them to that prospect. Damn them then
If ever mortal eyes do see them bolster
More than their own! What then? How then?
What shall I say? Where's satisfaction?
It is impossible you should see this,
Were they as prime as goats, as hot as monkeys,
As salt as wolves in pride, and fools as gross
As ignorance made drunk. But yet, I say,
If imputation and strong circumstance,
Which lead directly to the door of truth,
Will give you satisfaction, you might have't.
OTHELLO
Give me a living reason she's disloyal.
IAGO
I do not like the office.
But sith I am entered in this cause so far —
Pricked to't by foolish honesty and love —
I will go on. I lay with Cassio lately,
And being troubled with a raging tooth
I could not sleep.
There are a kind of men so loose of soul
That in their sleeps will mutter their affairs:
One of this kind is Cassio.
In sleep I heard him say: 'Sweet Desdemona,
Let us be wary, let us hide our loves';
And then, sir, would he gripe and wring my hand,
Cry 'O sweet creature!' and then kiss me hard,
As if he plucked up kisses by the roots,
That grew upon my lips; then laid his leg
Over my thigh, and sighed and kissed, and then
Cried 'Cursèd fate that gave thee to the Moor!'
OTHELLO
O monstrous! Monstrous!
IAGO   Nay, this was but his dream.

395　them：i. e. , Desdemona and Cassio.　**prospect**：sight, spectacle,景象。

396　bolster(v.)：share a bolster（长枕头）。

397　More：other.

400　prime：lustful.　**hot**：lecherous.

401　salt(adj.)：wanton, sensual.　**in pride**：in heat,发情。**gross**：sensual, obscene.

402　ignorance … drunk：喝醉的笨蛋。

406　living：tangible.

407　office：duty.

408　sith：since.

409　Pricked：spurred.

410　lay：was in bed.

411　raging tooth：toothache.

413　loose：unrestrained.

414　That：that they.

417　wary：cautious, watchful.　**loves**：伊丽莎白时代抽象名词可用复数。

418　gripe：grasp.

OTHELLO

425 But this denoted a foregone conclusion.

IAGO

'Tis a shrewd doubt, though it be but a dream:
And this may help to thicken other proofs
That do demonstrate thinly.

OTHELLO   I'll tear her all to pieces!

IAGO

Nay, but be wise: yet we see nothing done,
430 She may be honest yet. Tell me but this:
Have you not sometimes seen a handkerchief,
Spotted with strawberries, in your wife's hand?

OTHELLO

I gave her such a one: 'twas my first gift.

IAGO

I know not that: but such a handkerchief —
435 I am sure it was your wife's — did I today
See Cassio wipe his beard with.

OTHELLO   If it be that —

IAGO

If it be that, or any that was hers,
It speaks against her with the other proofs.

OTHELLO

O, that the slave had forty thousand lives!
440 One is too poor, too weak for my revenge.
Now do I see 'tis true. Look here, Iago —
All my fond love thus do I blow to heaven:
'Tis gone.

Arise, black vengeance, from thy hollow cell!
445 Yield up, O love, thy crown and hearted throne
To tyrannous hate! Swell, bosom, with thy fraught,
For 'tis of aspics' tongues!

IAGO   Yet be content.

OTHELLO

ACT III SCENE III

425 foregone conclusion: earlier experience.

426 shrewd doubt: grievous suspicion.

427 thicken: strengthen.

432 Spotted: marked with a color different from the ground, embroidered.

439 the slave: 指 Cassio.

442 fond: foolish.

445 Yield up: give up.　　**hearted throne**: throne in men's hearts.

446 fraught(n.): load, freight.

447 'tis of: my bosom is full of.　　**aspics' tongues**: tongues of poisonous snakes.　　**be content**: be quiet, be calm.

O, blood, blood, blood!

IAGO

Patience, I say: your mind perhaps may change.

OTHELLO

450 Never, Iago. Like to the Pontic sea,
Whose icy current and compulsive course
Ne'er feels retiring ebb, but keeps due on
To the Propontic and the Hellespont,
Even so my bloody thoughts with violent pace
455 Shall ne'er look back, ne'er ebb to humble love,
Till that a capable and wide revenge
Swallow them up. Now, by yond marble heaven,
In the due reverence of a sacred vow
I here engage my words.

He kneels

IAGO   Do not rise yet.

He kneels

460 Witness you ever-burning lights above,
You elements, that clip us round about,
Witness that here Iago doth give up
The execution of his wit, hands, heart,
To wronged Othello's service. Let him command,
465 And to obey shall be in me remorse,
What bloody business ever.

They rise

OTHELLO   I greet thy love,
Not with vain thanks, but with acceptance bounteous;
And will upon the instant put thee to't.
Within these three days let me hear thee say
That Cassio's not alive.

470 IAGO   My friend is dead;
'Tis done at your request. But let her live.

OTHELLO

Damn her, lewd minx! O, damn her, damn her!

ACT III SCENE III

450 **Like to**: like. **Pontic sea**: Black Sea.

451 **compulsive**: driving onward.

452 **due on**: right on.

453 **Propontic**: Sea of Marmora. **Hellespont**: Dardanelles,达达尼尔海峡。

456 **capable**: capacious, comprehensive.

457 **them**: 指 Desdemona 和 Cassio. **yond**: yonder, over there. **marble**: radiant, shining.

458 **due**: proper. **reverence**: high respect.

459 **engage**: pledge.

460 **Witness you**: 请你们作见证(为祈使句)。 **ever-burning lights**: sun, moon and stars.

461 **elements**: natural elements: earth, water, air, fire. **clip**: encompass.

462 **give up**: devote, dedicate.

463 **execution**: exercise, action. **wit**: mind.

465 **remorse**: solemn obligation.

468 **upon the instant**: instantly, at once. **put thee to't**: put your promise to the proof.

472 **minx**: pert and wanton woman.

Come go with me apart. I will withdraw
To furnish me with some swift means of death
475 For the fair devil. Now art thou my Lieutenant.
IAGO
I am your own for ever. *Exeunt*

SCENE IV

III. iv *Enter Desdemona, Emilia, and Clown*

DESDEMONA Do you know, sirrah, where Lieutenant Cassio lies?

CLOWN I dare not say he lies anywhere.

DESDEMONA Why, man?

5 CLOWN He's a soldier, and for one to say a soldier lies is stabbing.

DESDEMONA Go to! Where lodges he?

CLOWN To tell you where he lodges is to tell you where I lie.

10 DESDEMONA Can anything be made of this?

CLOWN I know not where he lodges, and for me to devise a lodging, and say he lies here, or he lies there, were to lie in mine own throat.

DESDEMONA Can you inquire him out? And be edified by
15 report?

CLOWN I will catechize the world for him, that is, make questions, and by them answer.

DESDEMONA Seek him; bid him come hither; tell him I have moved my lord on his behalf, and hope all will be
20 well.

CLOWN To do this is within the compass of man's wit, and therefore I will attempt the doing of it. *Exit*

DESDEMONA

Where should I lose that handkerchief, Emilia?

EMILIA

474　furnish me：provide myself.

III. iv

1　sirrah：ordinary form of address to inferiors.

2　lies：lodges, stays.

3　lies：tells lies（小丑玩弄双关语的游戏）。

4　man：form of address to a servant.

6　stabbing：killing,性命攸关的事。

7　Go to：come,得了(是一种责备或告诫的语句)。

9　lie：扯谎。

14—15　inquire him out：打听他的住处。　　**edified by report**：enlightened (instructed) by information.

16　catechize：作(基督教的)教义提问,询问。

19　moved：influenced, persuaded.

21　within the compass：within the scope.

I know not, madam.

DESDEMONA

25 Believe me, I had rather have lost my purse
Full of crusadoes; and, but my noble Moor
Is true of mind, and made of no such baseness
As jealous creatures are, it were enough
To put him to ill-thinking.

EMILIA   Is he not jealous?

DESDEMONA

30 Who? He? I think the sun where he was born
Drew all such humours from him.

EMILIA   Look where he comes.

Enter Othello

DESDEMONA

I will not leave him now till Cassio
Be called to him. How is't with you, my lord?

OTHELLO

Well, my good lady. (*Aside*) O, hardness to dissemble!

35 How do you, Desdemona?

DESDEMONA   Well, my good lord.

OTHELLO

Give me your hand. This hand is moist, my lady.

DESDEMONA

It yet has felt no age, nor known no sorrow.

OTHELLO

This argues fruitfulness and liberal heart.
Hot, hot and moist. This hand of yours requires
40 A sequester from liberty, fasting and prayer,
Much castigation, exercise devout;
For there's a young and sweating devil here
That commonly rebels. 'Tis a good hand,
A frank one.

DESDEMONA   You may, indeed, say so;

26 crusadoes: Portuguese gold coins.　**but**: but for the fact that.
28 are: i. e. , are made of.　**were**: would be.
31 humours: 体液。中世纪欧洲人认为人有四种体液: blood, phlegn, choler, black bile, 因其不平衡而产生人的不同。
33 called: recalled.
34 hardness to dissemble: how difficult to pretend.
35 How do you: How are you.　**Well**: I am well.
36 moist: moist as a sign of lust, but Desdemona responds to its alternative meaning, that of indicating youthfulness.
38 argues: betokens, gives evidence of.　**liberal**: generous, but also licentious.
40 sequester: separation.　**liberty**: licentious thoughts.
41 castigation: 天主教的一种净心、禁欲和苦修。　**exercise devout**: devout exercise (worship), 虔诚, 礼拜。
44 frank: free, open, sexually unrestrained.

45　　　For 'twas that hand that gave away my heart.
OTHELLO
　　　A liberal hand! The hearts of old gave hands;
　　　But our new heraldry is hands, not hearts.
DESDEMONA
　　　I cannot speak of this. Come now, your promise.
OTHELLO
　　　What promise, chuck?
DESDEMONA
50　　　I have sent to bid Cassio come speak with you.
OTHELLO
　　　I have a salt and sorry rheum offends me;
　　　Lend me thy handkerchief.
DESDEMONA　　　　　　　　　　Here, my lord.
OTHELLO
　　　That which I gave you.
DESDEMONA　　　　　　　I have it not about me.
OTHELLO
　　　Not?
DESDEMONA No, faith, my lord.
OTHELLO　　　　　　　　　　　　That is a fault.
55　　　That handkerchief
　　　Did an Egyptian to my mother give;
　　　She was a charmer and could almost read
　　　The thoughts of people. She told her, while she kept it,
　　　'Twould make her amiable and subdue my father
60　　　Entirely to her love; but, if she lost it
　　　Or made a gift of it, my father's eye
　　　Should hold her loathèd, and his spirits should hunt
　　　After new fancies. She, dying, gave it me,
　　　And bid me, when my fate would have me wive,
65　　　To give it her. I did so; and take heed on't;
　　　Make it a darling, like your precious eye.
　　　To lose or give't away were such perdition

46 The … hands: once love went together with a promise of marriage. (英谚) give somebody one's hand,意为女子答应嫁给某人。

47 heraldry: emblem,纹章,表征。 **hands, not hearts**: 徒有结婚形式,而无爱。

48 I … this: I do not understand what you are talking about.

49 chuck: 小鸡,a term of affection.

51 salt: 指伤风流鼻涕、眼泪等,内含盐分。 **sorry**: serious, bad. **rheum**: 流鼻涕的伤风。 **offends**: (其前省去 which) annoys, pains.

54 faith: in faith, honestly.

56 Egyptian: gypsy,吉卜赛人。罗姆人原为印度贱民,15世纪辗转来到欧洲,由于经埃及而来,被误为埃及人,脱落首字母,变为 gypsy 人。

57 charmer: sorceress, witch,女巫。

59 amiable: lovable.

62 hold: regard her as.

64 bid: 是当时 bid 的过去式。 **wive**: marry.

65 take heed on't: take care of it.

67 were: would be. **perdition**: loss, ruin.

　　　　As nothing else could match.
DESDEMONA　　　　　　　Is't possible?
OTHELLO
　　'Tis true; there's magic in the web of it.
70　A sibyl, that had numbered in the world
　　The sun to course two hundred compasses,
　　In her prophetic fury sewed the work;
　　The worms were hallowed that did breed the silk,
　　And it was dyed in mummy, which the skilful
75　Conserved of maidens' hearts.
DESDEMONA　　　　　　Indeed! Is't true?
OTHELLO
　　Most veritable; therefore look to't well.
DESDEMONA
　　Then would to God that I had never seen it!
OTHELLO
　　Ha! Wherefore?
DESDEMONA
　　Why do you speak so startingly and rash?
OTHELLO
80　Is't lost? Is't gone? Speak; is't out o'th'way?
DESDEMONA
　　Heaven bless us!
OTHELLO　　　　Say you?
DESDEMONA　　　　　　It is not lost.
　　But what an if it were?
OTHELLO　　　　　　How!
DESDEMONA
　　I say it is not lost.
OTHELLO　　　　　Fetch't; let me see't.
DESDEMONA
　　Why, so I can, sir; but I will not now.
85　This is a trick to put me from my suit.
　　Pray you let Cassio be received again.

68 match: be a counterpart.
69 web: fabric, texture.
70 sibyl: 希腊神话中女预言家之一。
71 course ... compasses: run two hundred circles, 意谓活了两百年。
72 fury: inspired frenzy.
73 worms: silkworms, 蚕。 **hallowed**: made holy, consecrated.
74 mummy: 木乃伊制剂。 **the skilful**: those who are skilled in magical arts.
75 Conserved of: prepared from.
76 veritable: true. **look to't well**: take good care of it.
77 would: I wish.
78 wherefore: for what reason.
79 startingly: startlingly, in a frightening manner. **rash**(adv.): hastily, rudely, 粗野地。
80 out o'th' way: mislaid, missing.
81 Say you?: What do you say to it?
85 put me from: divert from.

OTHELLO

Fetch me the handkerchief: my mind misgives.

DESDEMONA

Come, come:
You'll never meet a more sufficient man.

OTHELLO

The handkerchief!

90 DESDEMONA   I pray, talk me of Cassio.

OTHELLO

The handkerchief!

DESDEMONA   A man that all his time
Hath founded his good fortunes on your love;
Shared dangers with you —

OTHELLO

The handkerchief!

DESDEMONA   I'faith you are to blame.

OTHELLO

95 Zounds!

EMILIA

Is not this man jealous?

DESDEMONA   I ne'er saw this before.
Sure, there's some wonder in this handkerchief:
I am most unhappy in the loss of it.

EMILIA

'Tis not a year or two shows us a man.
100   They are all but stomachs, and we all but food;
They eat us hungerly, and when they are full,
They belch us. Look you, Cassio and my husband.
        Enter Iago and Cassio

IAGO

There is no other way: 'tis she must do't.
And lo, the happiness! Go, and importune her.

DESDEMONA

105 How now, good Cassio! What's the news with you?

87 misgives: has a presentiment of evil, 预感坏事即将来临。
89 sufficient: fit, able.
90 talk me of: talk to me about.
91 all his time: throughout his career.
97 wonder: magic.
99 'Tis ... man: it does not take more than a couple of years to show up to us the nature of a man.
100 all but: nothing but.
101 hungerly: hungrily.
102 belch: spit out.
103 must: who must（用 it is 或 there is 开头的句子,其表语（或主语）后的定语从句常省掉作主语的关系代词）。
104 the happiness: happily met.

CASSIO
Madam, my former suit. I do beseech you
That by your virtuous means I may again
Exist and be a member of his love,
Whom I, with all the office of my heart,
Entirely honour. I would not be delayed.
If my offence be of such mortal kind
That nor my service past, nor present sorrow,
Nor purposed merit in futurity,
Can ransom me into his love again,
But to know so must be my benefit;
So shall I clothe me in a forced content,
And shut myself up in some other course
To Fortune's alms.

DESDEMONA　　　　Alas, thrice-gentle Cassio!
My advocation is not now in tune;
My lord is not my lord; nor should I know him,
Were he in favour as in humour altered.
So help me every spirit sanctified
As I have spoken for you all my best,
And stood within the blank of his displeasure
For my free speech! You must awhile be patient.
What I can do, I will; and more I will,
Than for myself I dare. Let that suffice you.

IAGO
Is my lord angry?

EMILIA　　　　　　He went hence but now
And certainly in strange unquietness.

IAGO
Can he be angry? I have seen the cannon
When it hath blown his ranks into the air,
And like the devil from his very arm
Puffed his own brother — and can he be angry?
Something of moment then. I will go meet him.

ACT III SCENE IV

107 virtuous: efficacious.

109 Whom: 指上文 his love, 即 the love of him 中的 him. **office**: loyal service.

111 mortal: fatal.

112 nor ... nor: neither ... nor.

113 Nor ... futurity: nor the merit I intend to get in the futurity.

114 ransom: bring by ransoming.

115 to ... benefit: it must be to my benefit to know so (that my case is hopeless).

116 clothe ... content: cover myself in a willy-nilly content, i. e., make the best of a bad situation. **content**: satisfaction, contentedness.

117 shut myself up: 死心塌地地采取。

118 To Fortune's alms: at the mercy of fortune.

119 advocation: advocacy, pleading. **in tune**: in harmony, 悦耳。

121 favour ... altered: as changed in appearance as in temper.

124 blank: bull's eye, 靶心的白点。

125 For: on account of. **free**: open, frank.

131 blown his ranks: shot his soldiers to pieces.

132 from his very arm: just beside him.

133 Puffed: blown up.

134 moment: importance.

135   There's matter in't indeed if he be angry.
DESDEMONA
       I prithee do so.   *Exit Iago*
                        Something, sure, of state,
       Either from Venice, or some unhatched practice
       Made demonstrable here in Cyprus to him,
       Hath puddled his clear spirirt; and in such cases
140   Men's natures wrangle with inferior things,
       Though great ones arc their object. 'Tis even so.
       For let our finger ache, and it endues
       Our healthful members even to that sense
       Of pain. Nay, we must think men are not gods,
145   Nor of them look for such observancy
       As fits the bridal. Beshrew me much, Emilia,
       I was — unhandsome warrior as I am —
       Arraigning his unkindness with my soul;
       But now I find I had suborned the witness
150   And he's indicted falsely.
EMILIA
       Pray heaven it be state matters, as you think,
       And no conception nor no jealous toy
       Concerning you.
DESDEMONA
       Alas the day, I never gave him cause.
EMILIA
155   But jealous souls will not be answered so;
       They are not ever jealous for the cause,
       But jealous for they're jealous. It is a monster
       Begot upon itself, born on itself.
DESDEMONA
       Heaven keep that monster from Othello's mind.
EMILIA
160   Lady, amen!
DESDEMONA

136 **Something of state**: 国家的政事。

137 **unhatched practice**: unexecuted plot.

138 **demonstrable**: evident, apparent.

139 **puddled**: muddled.

140 **inferior**: petty, trifling.

142 **endues**: induces, leads to.

143 **members**: limbs.

145 **of**: from.　**observancy**: attention, 殷勤体贴。

146 **bridal**: wedding day, honeymoon.　**Beshrew me**: curse me (温和的赌咒语)。

147 **unhandsome warrior**: clumsy soldier.

148 **Arraigning**: calling to account, accusing(法律用语)。　**with**: before the bar (i.e. court) of.

149 **suborned**: bribed, corrupted.

152 **nor no**: 双重否定。　**toy**: fancy.

154 **Alas the day**: 感叹语。

157 **for**: because.　**It is a monster**: 参看 III. iii 164。

160 **amen**: 基督教祈祷常用语,表示赞同某个祝愿。

    I will go seek him. Cassio, walk here about.
    If I do find him fit, I'll move your suit,
    And seek to effect it to my uttermost.

CASSIO

    I humbly thank your ladyship.

Exeunt Desdemona and Emilia

Enter Bianca

BIANCA

165   'Save you, friend Cassio.

CASSIO   What make you from home?
    How is it with you, my most fair Bianca?
    I'faith, sweet love, I was coming to your house.

BIANCA

    And I was going to your lodging, Cassio.
    What! Keep a week away? Seven days and nights?
170 Eight score eight hours? And lovers' absent hours
    More tedious than the dial eight score times!
    O weary reckoning!

CASSIO   Pardon me, Bianca.
    I have this while with leaden thoughts been pressed;
    But I shall in a more continuate time
175 Strike off this score of absence. Sweet Bianca,
    Take me this work out.

BIANCA   O Cassio, whence came this?
    This is some token from a newer friend.
    To the felt absence now I feel a cause.
    Is't come to this? Well, well.

CASSIO   Go to, woman!
180 Throw your vile guesses in the devil's teeth
    From whence you have them. You are jealous now
    That this is from some mistress, some remembrance;
    No, by my faith, Bianca.

BIANCA   Why, whose is it?

CASSIO

162 **fit**: in a suitable mood.　**move**: plead.

165 **'Save you**: (招呼语) God save you.　**What … home?**: What are you doing, away from home?

171 **dial**: 钟表走的时间。　**eight score times**: 8×20 倍, 此短语正常位置在 More 之前。

173 **this while**: all the time.　**leaden**: heavy, 沉重如铅。

174 **continuate**: uninterrupted.

175 **score**: 欠账。

176 **Take … out**: copy this pattern for me (交手绢)。

177 **friend**: mistress.

178 **felt**: keenly sensible of.　**feel**: perceive.

179 **Go to**: away with you.

182 **remembrance**: souvenir.

I know not, sweet. I found it in my chamber.
I like the work well. Ere it be demanded —
As like enough it will — I'd have it copied.
Take it and do't, and leave me for this time.
BIANCA
Leave you? Wherefore?
CASSIO
I do attend here on the General,
And think it no addition, nor my wish,
To have him see me womaned.
BIANCA   Why, I pray you?
CASSIO
Not that I love you not.
BIANCA   But that you do not love me.
I pray you, bring me on the way a little,
And say if I shall see you soon at night.
CASSIO
'Tis but a little way that I can bring you,
For I attend here; but I'll see you soon.
BIANCA
'Tis very good; I must be circumstanced.   *Exeunt*

185 **Ere:** before.   **demanded:** wanted back.
186 **like:** likely.
189 **attend on:** wait for.
190 **addition:** credit.
191 **womaned:** accompanied by a woman.
193 **bring:** accompany.
197 **be circumstanced:** be governed by circumstance, i. e., yield to your conditions.

ACT IV

SCENE I

IV. i   *Enter Othello and Iago*

IAGO

  Will you think so?
OTHELLO   Think so, Iago?
IAGO   What!
  To kiss in private?
OTHELLO   An unauthorized kiss.
IAGO
  Or to be naked with her friend in bed
  An hour or more, not meaning any harm?
OTHELLO
5 Naked in bed, Iago, and not mean harm?
  It is hypocrisy against the devil.
  They that mean virtuously and yet do so,
  The devil their virtue tempts, and they tempt heaven.
IAGO
  So they do nothing, 'tis a venial slip.
10 But if I give my wife a handkerchief —
OTHELLO
  What then?
IAGO
  Why, then, 'tis hers, my lord, and being hers,
  She may, I think, bestow't on any man.
OTHELLO
  She is protectress of her honour too.
15 May she give that?
IAGO

IV. i

2 **unauthorized**: illicit.

6 **hypocrisy against the devil**: playing a false part to cheat the devil.

7 **They that**: those who.   **do so**: i. e. , be naked in bed together.

8 **tempts**: entice to evil.   **tempt**: defy, provoke.

9 **So**: so long as.   **venial slip**: pardonable mistake.

14 **protectress**: female protector.

Her honour is an essence that's not seen;
They have it very oft that have it not.
But for the handkerchief —

OTHELLO

By heaven, I would most gladly have forgot it!
Thou said'st — O, it comes o'er my memory
As doth the raven o'er the infected house,
Boding to all! — he had my handkerchief.

IAGO

Ay, what of that?

OTHELLO   That's not so good now.

IAGO   What
If I had said, I had seen him do you wrong,
Or heard him say — as knaves be such abroad,
Who having by their own importunate suit
Or voluntary dotage of some mistress
Convincèd or supplied them, cannot choose
But they must blab —

OTHELLO   Hath he said anything?

IAGO

He hath, my lord; but be you well assured,
No more than he'll unswear.

OTHELLO   What hath he said?

IAGO

Faith, that he did — I know not what he did.

OTHELLO

What? What?

IAGO

Lie —

OTHELLO With her?

IAGO   With her, on her, what you will.

OTHELLO Lie with her? Lie on her? We say lie on her when they belie her. Lie with her! Zounds, that's fulsome! Handkerchief — confession — handkerchief! To

16　honour：除抽象的"荣誉"外，也可理解为 maidenhood, chastity, 贞操。　**essence**：essential quality.

17　They … not：Those who have lost their chastity often seem to have it still, since chastity is an invisible essence.

18　for：as for.

19　forgot：forgotten.

21　raven：食腐肉的黑老鸹。　**infected house**：house infected with plague.

22　Boding to all：auguring evil to every member of the house.

25　knaves be such：these are such knaves.　**abroad**：at large, everywhere.

26　importunate suit：ardent wooing.

27　voluntary … mistress：情妇的自动垂青。　**dotage**：foolish affection.

28　Convincèd：overcome, seduced.　**supplied**：satisfied, gratified.　**them**：i. e., the mistresses.

29　blab：talk much, brag.

31　unswear：swear denial of, 发誓否认。

32　Faith：in faith.　**did**：做了那件事。

34　what you will：as you wish.

35　lie：双关语 1. 前面几个 lie 意为躺卧；2. 最后一个 lie 意为说谎。

36—37　they：系泛指的主语，与泛指的 we 或 you 无异。　**belie**：tell lies about.　**Zounds**：Christ's wounds（为赌咒语）。　**fulsome**：disgusting.

confess and be hanged for his labour. First to be hanged and then to confess! I tremble at it. Nature would not invest herself in such shadowing passion without some instruction. It is not words that shakes me thus! Pish! Noses, ears, and lips! Is't possible? — Confess? Handkerchief! O devil!

He falls

IAGO

Work on,
My medicine, work! Thus credulous fools are caught,
And many worthy and chaste dames even thus,
All guiltless, meet reproach. What ho, my lord!
My lord, I say! Othello!

Enter Cassio

How now, Cassio!

CASSIO

What's the matter?

IAGO

My lord is fallen into an epilepsy.
This is his second fit; he had one yesterday.

CASSIO

Rub him about the temples.

IAGO   No, forbear.
The lethargy must have his quiet course.
If not, he foams at mouth; and by and by
Breaks out to savage madness. Look, he stirs.
Do you withdraw yourself a little while;
He will recover straight. When he is gone,
I would on great occasion speak with you.

Exit Cassio

How is it, General? Have you not hurt your head?

OTHELLO

Dost thou mock me?

IAGO   I mock you? No, by heaven!

38 confess and be hanged：(英谚)在绞架旁对囚犯说的话。 **labour**：trouble, pains taken (in making the confession). **his**：指 Cassio. 接下去奥瑟罗把次序颠倒,先吊死后忏悔,说明他开始语无伦次。

39—41 Nature ... instruction：Nature would not dress (present) herself in such passionate imaginings unless for some instructive purpose.

41—42 words：i. e., mere words. 谓语用单数,是不规则的。 **shakes me**：makes me tremble. **Pish**：呸(表示轻蔑或厌恶的感叹词)。

42 Noses, ears, lips!：摸鼻子,咬耳朵,吮嘴唇!

46 dames：ladies, women.

47 reproach：disgrace.

50 epliepsy：癫痫。

52 temples：太阳穴。 **forbear**：stop.

53 lethargy：coma, 昏厥。 **have**：run. **his**：its.

54 by and by：before long.

57 straight：straight away, at once.

58 on great occasion：on some important matter.

59 Have ... head?：伊阿古带着厌恶讽刺的口吻问奥瑟罗是否患了戴绿头巾的头痛病。

60 Dost ... me?：i. e., as a cuckold.

Would you would bear your fortune like a man!
OTHELLO

A hornèd man's a monster and a beast.
IAGO

There's many a beast then in a populous city,
And many a civil monster.
OTHELLO

Did he confess it?

65 IAGO   Good sir, be a man.
Think every bearded fellow that's but yoked
May draw with you. There's millions now alive
That nightly lie in those unproper beds
Which they dare swear peculiar. Your case is better.
70 O, 'tis the spite of hell, the fiend's arch-mock,
To lip a wanton in a secure couch,
And to suppose her chaste! No, let me know;
And knowing what I am, I know what shall be.
OTHELLO

O, thou art wise, 'tis certain.
IAGO   Stand you awhile apart;
75 Confine yourself but in a patient list.
Whilst you were here, o'erwhelmèd with your grief —
A passion most unsuiting such a man —
Cassio came hither. I shifted him away
And laid good scuse upon your ecstasy;
80 Bade him anon return and here speak with me,
The which he promised. Do but encave yourself,
And mark the fleers, the gibes, and notable scorns
That dwell in every region of his face.
For I will make him tell the tale anew,
85 Where, how, how oft, how long ago, and when
He hath, and is again, to cope your wife.
I say, but mark his gestures. Marry, patience!
Or I shall say you're all in all in spleen

61 Would you would: I wish you would.

62 hornèd man: 头上长角的人,受骗的丈夫。

64 civil: polite, well-mannered, 体面的,文明的。

66 yoked: i. e., married.

67 draw: pull a vehicle (接 yoke 的譬喻),转意 act in concert. **There's**: there are.

68 unproper: not belonging exclusively to anyone, common.

69 dare: have boldness to. **peculiar**: their own, private. **Your case is better**: i. e., because you know the truth.

70 spite: mortification, 折磨。 **arch-mock**: supreme joke.

71 lip (v. t.): kiss. **wanton**: loose woman. **secure couch**: bed supposedly safe from others.

73 what I am: i. e., a cuckold. **what shall be**: what I shall be.

74 wise: 有多种意思:明智的,知情的,神经正常的。

75 in a patient list: within the bounds of list, 原意为一块围起来的竞技场。

78 shifted him away: contrived to send him away.

79 scuse: excuse. **ecstasy**: trance, swoon.

81 encave: hide.

82 fleers: sneers, look of contempt. **gibes**: taunts. **notable**: noticeable, obvious.

86 cope (v. t.): 有多种解释:meet, encounter, tackle, cover.

87 Marry: by Virgin Mary(赌咒语)。

88 all in all: completely. **spleen**: bad temper, anger. spleen 原意为脾脏,中世纪认为脾脏是人的愤怒和忧郁等情绪的发源地。

And nothing of a man.

OTHELLO   Dost thou hear, Iago?
90 I will be found most cunning in my patience,
But — dost thou hear? — most bloody.

IAGO   That's not amiss,
But yet keep time in all. Will you withdraw?

Othello retires

Now will I question Cassio of Bianca,
A housewife, that by selling her desires
95 Buys herself bread and clothes. It is a creature
That dotes on Cassio — as 'tis the strumpet's plague
To beguile many and be beguiled by one.
He, when he hears of her, cannot refrain
From the excess of laughter. Here he comes.
   Enter Cassio
100 As he shall smile, Othello shall go mad;
And his unbookish jealousy must construe
Poor Cassio's smiles, gestures, and light behaviour
Quite in the wrong. How do you now, Lieutenant?

CASSIO

The worser that you give me the addition
105 Whose want even kills me.

IAGO

Ply Desdemona well and you are sure on't.
Now if this suit lay in Bianca's power,
How quickly should you speed!

CASSIO   Alas, poor caitiff!

OTHELLO

(*aside*) Look, how he laughs already!

IAGO
110 I never knew a woman love man so.

CASSIO

Alas, poor rogue! I think i'faith she loves me.

OTHELLO

89　nothing of a man: 没有一点大丈夫气概。

90　cunning: clever, ingenious.

91　bloody: bloodthirsty, 有杀心。

92　keep time in all: keep yourself steady in everything, 凡事沉住气。

93　of: about.

94　housewife: hussy, prostitute.

96　dotes on: loves to excess.　**strumpet**: prostitute.　**plague**: trouble, affliction, 报应, 晦气。

97　beguile: deceive, cheat.

101　his: i. e., Othello's.　**unbookish**: ignorant, uninstructed.　**construe**: interpret.

102　light behaviour: wanton conduct, 轻浮的举止。

103　How do you now: How are you (doing) now? 你好么？

104　The worser that …: that 引导的从句(或 for 短语)用在 that +比较级之后表原因。

105　want (n.): lack, deprivation.

106　ply: urge, importune, 一再请求。　**on't**: of it.

108　speed: succeed.　**caitiff**: miserable person.

111　rogue: mischevous person (as term of endearment).

(*aside*) Now he denies it faintly, and laughs it out.
IAGO
  Do you hear, Cassio?
OTHELLO
  (*aside*) Now he importunes him to tell it o'er.
  Go to, well said, well said!
IAGO
  She gives it out that you shall marry her.
  Do you intend it?
CASSIO
  Ha, ha, ha!
OTHELLO
  (*aside*) Do you triumph, Roman? Do you triumph?
CASSIO I marry her! What! A customer! Prithee bear some charity to my wit: do not think it so unwholesome. Ha, ha, ha!
OTHELLO (*aside*) So, so, so, so: they laugh that win.
IAGO Faith, the cry goes that you shall marry her.
CASSIO Prithee, say true.
IAGO I am a very villain else.
OTHELLO (*aside*) Have you scored me? Well.
CASSIO This is the monkey's own giving out. She is persuaded I will marry her out of her own love and flattery, not out of my promise.
OTHELLO (*aside*) Iago beckons me. Now he begins the story.
CASSIO She was here even now. She haunts me in every place. I was the other day talking on the sea-bank with certain Venetians, and thither comes the bauble and, by this hand, falls me thus about my neck.
OTHELLO (*aside*) Crying 'O dear Cassio!' as it were. His gesture imports it.
CASSIO So hangs and lolls and weeps upon me, so hales and pulls me. Ha, ha, ha!

112　faintly: half-heartedly.

115　Go to: come, 好啦, 得啦。　**well said**: well done.

116　gives it out: spreads the word.

119　triumph(v.i.): 得意扬扬。　**Roman**: 罗马人得胜时惯于举行凯旋游行。

120—122　I marry her: 'marry' 为 bare infinitive, 主语后不带 to 的不定式, 表惊奇于不可能之事。　**customer**: prostitute.　**Prithee**: I pray you to.　**bear … wit**: be more charitable to (in estimating) intelligence.　**it**: 指 my wit.　**unwholesome**: tainted, defective.

124　Faith: in faith, really, indeed.　**cry**: rumour.

125　true (adv.): truthfully.

126　else: otherwise, i.e., if I don't say true.

127　scored me: ①branded or beaten me; ②set down my reckoning or settled accounts with me.

128　the monkey: Cassio 对 Bianca 的戏谑称呼。

129　out of: from, on the strength of.

130　flattery: self-flattery.

131　beckons: signals to.

133　haunts me: follows me persistently, 缠着我。

135　certain: some.　**bauble**: childish person 原意为小玩意儿。

136　by this hand: 用我的这只手起誓。　**me**: 语法上叫泛指人称 (ethical dative), 为了使语言生动而用, 无词汇意义。　**falls … about**: 挽住, 抱住。

138　imports it: conveys the meaning.

139　lolls: leans, reclines.

140　hales: drags.

OTHELLO (*aside*) Now he tells how she plucked him to my chamber. O, I see that nose of yours, but not that dog I shall throw it to!

CASSIO Well, I must leave her company.

IAGO Before me! Look where she comes.

CASSIO 'Tis such another fitchew! Marry, a perfumed one!

Enter Bianca

What do you mean by this haunting of me?

BIANCA Let the devil and his dam haunt you! What did you mean by that same handkerchief you gave me even now? I was a fine fool to take it. I must take out the work! A likely piece of work, that you should find it in your chamber, and not know who left it there! This is some minx's token, and I must take out the work? There, give it your hobby-horse, wheresoever you had it. I'll take out no work on't.

CASSIO How now, my sweet Bianca! How now, how now!

OTHELLO (*aside*) By heaven, that should be my handkerchief!

BIANCA If you'll come to supper tonight, you may. If you will not, come when you are next prepared for.

Exit

IAGO After her, after her!

CASSIO Faith I must: she'll rail in the street else.

IAGO Will you sup there?

CASSIO Faith, I intend to.

IAGO Well, I may chance to see you: for I would very fain speak with you.

CASSIO Prithee come, will you?

IAGO Go to! Say no more.   *Exit Cassio*

OTHELLO (*coming forward*) How shall I murder him, Iago?

141　plucked: drew, pulled.

145　Before me: on my soul, 起誓语。

146　fitchew: polecat, thought to be very amorous, hence a wanton woman, 骚货。

148　dam: mother.

150　fine: great, big.　**take out**: take a copy of.

151　likely piece of work: fine story.

153　minx: a pert and wanton woman, 小荡妇。

154　hobby-horse: term of contempt for a harlot or a loose woman. 原意为英国民间舞蹈中扎在腰间的柳条马。

157　should be: must be.

160　when you are next prepared for: when next I am ready for you (i.e. never).

162　Faith: in faith, indeed.　**rail**: scold, shout abuses, 谩骂。**else**: otherwise.

165　chance: happen.　**would very fain**: would be very glad to.

168　Go to: expression of remonstrance.

170 IAGO Did you perceive how he laughed at his vice?
OTHELLO O, Iago!
IAGO And did you see the handkerchief?
OTHELLO Was that mine?
IAGO Yours, by this hand! And to see how he prizes the
175 foolish woman your wife: she gave it him, and he hath giv'n it his whore.
OTHELLO I would have him mine years a-killing! — A fine woman, a fair woman, a sweet woman!
IAGO Nay, you must forget that.
180 OTHELLO Ay, let her rot and perish, and be damned tonight, for she shall not live! No, my heart is turned to stone: I strike it, and it hurts my hand. — O, the world hath not a sweeter creature! She might lie by an emperor's side and command him tasks.
185 IAGO Nay, that's not your way.
OTHELLO Hang her! I do but say what she is: so delicate with her needle, an admirable musician! O, she will sing the savageness out of a bear! Of so high and plenteous wit and invention!
190 IAGO She's the worse for all this.
OTHELLO O, a thousand, thousand times! — And then of so gentle a condition.
IAGO Ay, too gentle.
OTHELLO Nay, that's certain — but yet the pity of it, Iago!
195 O, Iago, the pity of it, Iago!
IAGO If you are so fond over her iniquity, give her patent to offend, for if it touch not you, it comes near nobody.
OTHELLO I will chop her into messes! Cuckold me!
200 IAGO O, 'tis foul in her!
OTHELLO With mine officer!
IAGO That's fouler.

174　by this hand: i. e., I swear by my hand.

176　whore: prostitute.

177　have ... a-killing: spend nine years in the act of killing him.

184　command: cause to do.

185　your way: the way you should think of her.

189　invention: imagination, ingenuity.

192　of so gentle a condition: so well-born and well-bred.

193　gentle: generous, yielding (to men).

196　fond: 双关语 1. doting; 2. foolish.　**iniquity**: wickedness, sin.　**patent**: license.

197—198　offend: commit a fault or sin.　**touch**: affect, hurt. **it comes near nobody**: 不干别人的事。

199　messes: little piece of food.　**Cuckold me**: make me a cuckold （乌龟）。

OTHELLO Get me some poison, Iago, this night. I'll not expostulate with her, lest her body and beauty unprovide my mind again — this night, Iago.

IAGO Do it not with poison; strangle her in her bed, even the bed she hath contaminated.

OTHELLO Good, good! The justice of it pleases; very good!

IAGO And for Cassio, let me be his undertaker. You shall hear more by midnight.

OTHELLO

Excellent good!

Trumpet sounds

What trumpet is that same?

IAGO

I warrant, something from Venice.

Enter Lodovico, Desdemona, and attendants

'Tis Lodovico,

Come from the Duke; and see your wife is with him.

LODOVICO

God save you, worthy General!

OTHELLO   With all my heart, sir.

LODOVICO

The Duke and Senators of Venice greet you.

He gives him a letter

OTHELLO

I kiss the instrument of their pleasures.

He reads the letter

DESDEMONA

And what's the news, good cousin Lodovico?

IAGO

I am very glad to see you, signor:

Welcome to Cyprus.

LODOVICO

I thank you. How does Lieutenant Cassio?

204　expostulate：discuss.

205　unprovide：deprive of what is necessary, unnerse.

207　contaminated：tainted.

210　for：as for.　**undertaker**：dispatcher.

212　Excellent（adv.）：exceedingly.

213　I warrant：I'm sure.

214　Come（p. p.）：of come.

215　With all my heart：前省略 I welcome you.

217　instrument of：document conveying.　**pleasures**：orders, will,命令,意愿。

IAGO
　Lives, sir.
DESDEMONA
　Cousin, there's fallen between him and my lord
　An unkind breach; but you shall make all well.
OTHELLO
225　Are you sure of that?
DESDEMONA
　My lord?
OTHELLO
　'This fail you not to do, as you will' —
LODOVICO
　He did not call; he's busy in the paper.
　Is there division 'twixt my lord and Cassio?
DESDEMONA
230　A most unhappy one; I would do much
　T'atone them, for the love I bear to Cassio.
OTHELLO
　Fire and brimstone!
DESDEMONA
　My lord?
OTHELLO
　Are you wise?
DESDEMONA
　What, is he angry?
235　LODOVICO　　　　　　Maybe the letter moved him.
　For, as I think, they do command him home,
　Deputing Cassio in his government.
DESDEMONA
　By my troth, I am glad on't.
OTHELLO　　　　　　　　Indeed!
DESDEMONA　　　　　　　　　　My lord?
OTHELLO
　I am glad to see you mad.

223 **there's fallen**: there has happened.
224 **unkind**: unnatural, hurtful. **breach**: quarrel.
227 此行为 Othello 读信中文字,You must not fail to do this.
228 **busy**: engrossed.
229 **division**: disagreement.
231 **atone**: reconcile.
232 **Fire and brimstone**: Hell! (咒骂语)地狱中被认为充满火和硫黄。
234 **wise**: sane.
235 **moved**: agitated, disturbed.
237 **government**: office.
238 **troth**: faith. **on't**: of it.
239 **I am glad**: 对 Desdemona 学舌并反唇相讥。

DESDEMONA   Why, sweet Othello!
OTHELLO
240   Devil!

He strikes her

DESDEMONA

   I have not deserved this.

LODOVICO

   My lord, this would not be believed in Venice,
   Though I should swear I saw't. 'Tis very much.
   Make her amends; she weeps.

OTHELLO   O devil, devil!
245   If that the earth could teem with woman's tears,
   Each drop she falls would prove a crocodile.
   Out of my sight!

DESDEMONA   I will not stay to offend you.

LODOVICO

   Truly an obedient lady.
   I do beseech your lordship call her back.

OTHELLO
250   Mistress!

DESDEMONA

   My lord?

OTHELLO

   What would you with her, sir?

LODOVICO

   Who? I, my lord?

OTHELLO

   Ay, you did wish that I would make her turn.
255   Sir, she can turn, and turn, and yet go on,
   And turn again. And she can weep, sir, weep.
   And she's obedient; as you say, obedient,
   Very obedient — proceed you in your tears —
   Concerning this, sir — O, well-painted passion! —
260   I am commanded home — get you away!

243　very much：too much，过分。

244　Make her amends：compensate for her loss, i. e. , apologize to her.

245　If that：if.　**teem**：breed.

246　falls：lets fall.　**prove**：become.　**crocodile**：传说鳄鱼的眼泪都是假的。

250　Mistress：lady（反语）。

255　turn (v. i.)：do a turn (coition).

258　proceed you in：continue shedding.

259　well-painted：化装得很漂亮的，装腔作势的。　**passion**：i. e. , grief.

I'll send for you anon. — Sir, I obey the mandate,
And will return to Venice. — Hence, avaunt!

Exit Desdemona

Cassio shall have my place. And sir, tonight
I do entreat that we may sup together.
You are welcome, sir, to Cyprus. Goats and monkeys!

Exit

LODOVICO

Is this the noble Moor, whom our full senate
Call all-in-all sufficient? Is this the nature
Whom passion could not shake? Whose solid virtue
The shot of accident nor dart of chance
Could neither graze nor pierce?

IAGO   He is much changed.

LODOVICO

Are his wits safe? Is he not light of brain?

IAGO

He's that he is: I may not breathe my censure
What he might be. If what he might he is not,
I would to heaven he were.

LODOVICO   What! Strike his wife!

IAGO

Faith, that was not so well: yet would I knew
That stroke would prove the worst!

LODOVICO   Is it his use?
Or did the letters work upon his blood
And new-create this fault?

IAGO   Alas, alas!
It is not honesty in me to speak
What I have seen and known. You shall observe him,
And his own courses will denote him so,
That I may save my speech. Do but go after,
And mark how he continues.

LODOVICO

261 **mandate**: order.

262 **avaunt!**: (对 Desdemona)滚开!

265 **Goats and monkeys**: 均为淫荡的动物。参看 III. iii 419 行。

267 **all-in-all**: completely, absolutely. **sufficient**: able, capable.

268 **passion**: feeling, emotion.

269 **The ... chance**: 用 shot 和 dart 这两个具体名词使抽象名词 accident 和 chance 具体化,这是一种叫 reification 的修辞手法。

270 **graze**: 擦伤。

271 **Are his wits safe?**: Is he sober? 他神志清醒么? **light of brain**: light-headed, thoughtless, unsteady.

272 **that**: what.

274, 275 **would**: (I) wish.

276 **use**: habitual practice.

278 **new-create**: newly create.

281 **courses**: ways, behavior.

283 **mark**: take notice.

I am sorry that I am deceived in him.

SCENE II

IV. ii *Enter Othello and Emilia*

OTHELLO
You have seen nothing then?
EMILIA
Nor ever heard, nor ever did suspect.
OTHELLO
Yes, you have seen Cassio and she together.
EMILIA
But then I saw no harm; and then I heard
5 Each syllable that breath made up between them.
OTHELLO
What! Did they never whisper?
EMILIA   Never, my lord.
OTHELLO
Nor send you out o'th'way?
EMILIA   Never.
OTHELLO
To fetch her fan, her gloves, her mask, nor nothing?
EMILIA
Never, my lord.
OTHELLO
10 That's strange.
EMILIA
I durst, my lord, to wager she is honest,
Lay down my soul at stake. If you think other,
Remove your thought; it doth abuse your bosom.
If any wretch have put this in your head,
15 Let heaven requite it with the serpent's curse!
For if she be not honest, chaste, and true,
There's no man happy. The purest of their wives

284　am deceived in him：have misappraised him.

IV. ii

3　she：按现代语法为 her.

7　out o'th'way：out of the way.

8　nor nothing：or anything.

11　durst：古体 dare 的过去时,作假设语气用,如 would dare.

12　Lay … stake：用我的灵魂打赌。　　**other**：otherwise.

13　Remove your thought：stop thinking so.　　**abuse**：hurt, do harm to.　　**bosom**：thoughts, feelings.

15　requite：repay.　　**the serpent's curse**：见《圣经·旧约·创世记》第 3 章 14 节。魔鬼化的蛇引诱夏娃和亚当违背上帝意志之后,上帝诅咒蛇将用腹部行走,终生吃土。

Is foul as slander.

OTHELLO   Bid her come hither; go!

Exit Emilia

She says enough; yet she's a simple bawd
20 That cannot say as much. This is a subtle whore,
A closet lock and key of villainous secrets;
And yet she'll kneel and pray — I have seen her do't.
   Enter Desdemona and Emilia

DESDEMONA

My lord, what is your will?

OTHELLO   Pray, chuck, come hither.

DESDEMONA

What is your pleasure?

OTHELLO   Let me see your eyes.

Look in my face.

25 DESDEMONA What horrible fancy's this?

OTHELLO (*to Emilia*)

Some of your function, mistress.
Leave procreants alone and shut the door.
Cough or cry 'hem' if anybody come.
Your mystery, your mystery! Nay, dispatch!

Exit Emilia

DESDEMONA

30 Upon my knees, what doth your speech import?
I understand a fury in your words,
But not the words.

OTHELLO   Why, what art thou?

DESDEMONA

Your wife, my lord; your true and loyal wife.

OTHELLO

Come, swear it; damn thyself;
35 Lest being like one of heaven, the devils themselves
Should fear to seize thee. Therefore be doubledamned;
Swear thou art honest.

19—20 she's … much: any bawd (procuress) who can't say as much must be a simpleton.

20 This: 指 Desdemona. **subtle**: cunning.

21 closet lock and key: concealer.

23 chuck: chick (term of endearment).

26 Some of your function: go about your business, i.e., as a procuress.

27 procreants: mating couples.

29 mystery: profession, calling, trade. **dispatch**: be quick, hurry away.

34 damn thyself: 既诅咒忠实于丈夫而实际不忠实,就等于诅咒了自己必下地狱。

35 one of heaven: an angel.

DESDEMONA   Heaven doth truly know it.
OTHELLO

   Heaven truly knows that thou art false as hell.
DESDEMONA

   To whom, my lord? With whom? How am I false?
OTHELLO

40   Ah, Desdemona! Away, away, away!
DESDEMONA

   Alas, the heavy day! Why do you weep?
   Am I the motive of these tears, my lord?
   If haply you my father do suspect
   An instrument of this your calling back,
45   Lay not your blame on me. If you have lost him,
   I have lost him too.

   OTHELLO   Had it pleased heaven
   To try me with affliction, had they rained
   All kind of sores and shames on my bare head,
   Steeped me in poverty to the very lips,
50   Given to captivity me and my utmost hopes,
   I should have found in some place of my soul
   A drop of patience. But alas, to make me
   A fixèd figure for the time of scorn
   To point his slow unmoving finger at!
55   Yet could I bear that too, well, very well:
   But there where I have garnered up my heart,
   Where either I must live, or bear no life,
   The fountain from the which my current runs,
   Or else dries up — to be discarded thence
60   Or keep it as a cistern for foul toads
   To knot and gender in! Turn thy complexion there,
   Patience, thou young and rose-lipped cherubin,
   Ay, there look grim as hell!
DESDEMONA

   I hope my noble lord esteems me honest.

41 heavy: sad, sorrowful.

42 motive: cause.

43 haply: by hap, by chance, perhaps.   **suspect**: be ready to believe without ground.

44 instrument: means, agent.

47 try me with affliction: test me with suffering.   **they**: i. e., the heavenly powers.

48 sores: sicknesses, diseases.

49 Steeped: immersed, buried.

50 Given to captivity: captivate, arrest, restrain.

53 fixèd figure: permanent example (as the figure on the clock face).   **time of scorn**: scornful time, 时间拟人化。

54 his: its, 或理解为时间拟人化。   **slow unmoving**: 钟上的时针移动很慢, 好像静止一般。

56 garnered up my heart: stored the harvest of my love.

58 fountain: source, spring.   **the which**: which.

59 discarded: discharged.

60 cistern: pool, reservoir.

61 knot(v. i.): gather in a knot, copulate.   **gender**: breed.   **Turn thy complexion**: change thy colour, turn pale.

62 Patience: 为中世纪道德剧中"忍耐"角色, 意谓即使是她也会变色。   **cherubin**: angel.

64 esteems: thinks, considers.

OTHELLO

65   O, ay! As summer flies are in the shambles,
That quicken even with blowing, O, thou weed,
Who art so lovely fair, and smell'st so sweet
That the sense aches at thee, would thou hadst ne'er been born!

DESDEMONA

Alas, what ignorant sin have I committed?

OTHELLO

70   Was this fair paper, this most goodly book,
Made to write 'whore' upon? What committed!
Committed? O, thou public commoner!
I should make very forges of my cheeks,
That would to cinders burn up modesty,

75   Did I but speak thy deeds. What committed?
Heaven stops the nose at it, and the moon winks;
The bawdy wind, that kisses all it meets,
Is hushed within the hollow mine of earth
And will not hear it. What committed?
Impudent strumpet!

80   DESDEMONA   By heaven, you do me wrong.

OTHELLO

Are you not a strumpet?

DESDEMONA   No, as I am a Christian.

If to preserve this vessel for my lord
From any other foul unlawful touch,
Be not to be a strumpet, I am none.

OTHELLO

What! Not a whore?

85   DESDEMONA   No, as I shall be saved.

OTHELLO

Is't possible?

DESDEMONA

O, heaven forgive us!

65　shambles: slaughter-house.

66　quicken ... blowing: come to life as soon as the eggs are laid. **blowing** (v. i.): (of flies) deposit eggs.　**weed**: 可能指 thyme 百里香，见 I. iii 325 "weed up thyme".

69　what ... committed?: what sin have I committed ignorantly (in ignorance)? ignorant 为移位修饰语 transferred epithet

70　fair paper: i. e., the white body of Desdemona.

72　public commoner: one who offers herself to all comers.

73　I ... cheeks: i. e., If I told your deed, my cheeks would become as hot as a forge.

74　cinders: ashes.

76　stops the nose: holds its nose.　**winks**: shuts its eyes, as the moon symbolizes chastily.

77　bawdy: lewd.

78　hollow mine: cave. 传说风源于地洞。

79　it: what has been committed.

81　as I am a Christian: as sure as I am a Christian.

82　vessel: 容器,身体(见《圣经·新约·彼得前书》第 3 章 7 节,称妇女为 the weaker vessel).

85　as ... saved: as sure as I shall be saved.

OTHELLO I cry you mercy then:
I took you for that cunning whore of Venice
That married with Othello. (*Calling*) You, mistress,
That have the office opposite to Saint Peter
And keep the gate of hell!
  Enter Emilia
                              You, you, ay, you!
We have done our course: there's money for your pains.
I pray you turn the key, and keep our counsel. *Exit*

EMILIA
  Alas, what does this gentleman conceive?
  How do you, madam? How do you, my good lady?

DESDEMONA
  Faith, half asleep.

EMILIA
  Good madam, what's the matter with my lord?

DESDEMONA
  With who?

EMILIA
  Why, with my lord, madam.

DESDEMONA
  Who is thy lord?

EMILIA   He that is yours, sweet lady.

DESDEMONA
  I have none. Do not talk to me, Emilia:
  I cannot weep; nor answers have I none,
  But what should go by water. Prithee tonight
  Lay on my bed my wedding sheets, remember,
  And call thy husband hither

EMILIA   Here's a change indeed!
                                              Exit

DESDEMONA
  'Tis meet I should be used so, very meet.
  How have I been behaved, that he might stick

87　cry you mercy：beg your pardon.

90　office：job, work.　**opposite**：corresponding.　**Saint Peter**：见《圣经·新约·马太福音》第 16 章 19 节,为掌握天国大门钥匙的圣徒。

92　done our course：finished our talk or business.

93　keep our counsel：keep our affair secret.

94　conceive：form a plan in one's mind.

96　half asleep：dazed.

98　who：按现代语法应为 whom.

103　go by water：be expressed by tears.

106　meet：suitable, fitting (后省略 that).　**used**：treated.

107　been behaved：用被动态,等于 conducted myself. 参看现代的被动式 well-behaved.

The smallest opinion on my least misuse?
Enter Emilia and Iago

IAGO
What is your pleasure, madam? How is't with you?

DESDEMONA
I cannot tell: those that do teach young babes
Do it with gentle means and easy tasks;
He might have chid me so, for, in good faith,
I am a child to chiding.

IAGO   What is the matter, lady?

EMILIA
Alas, Iago, my lord hath so bewhored her,
Thrown such despite and heavy terms upon her
As true heart cannot bear.

DESDEMONA
Am I that name, Iago?

IAGO   What name, fair lady?

DESDEMONA
Such as she said my lord did say I was.

EMILIA
He called her whore: a beggar in his drink
Could not have laid such terms upon his callet.

IAGO
Why did he so?

DESDEMONA
I do not know: I am sure I am none such.

IAGO
Do not weep, do not weep. Alas the day!

EMILIA
Hath she forsook so many noble matches,
Her father, and her country, all her friends,
To be called whore? Would it not make one weep?

DESDEMONA
It is my wretched fortune.

ACT IV SCENE II

108 opinion: censure.　**misuse**: improper behaviour.
113 child: novice.
114 bewhored: called a whore.
115 despite: abuse, malice.　**heavy terms**: serious or harsh language.
119 in his drink: in his cups, 喝醉了的。
120 laid: applied.　**callet**: whore, trull.
124 forsook: forsaken.

IAGO   Beshrew him for't!
How comes this trick upon him?
DESDEMONA   Nay, heaven doth know.
EMILIA
I will be hanged if some eternal villain,
Some busy and insinuating rogue,
Some cogging, cozening slave, to get some office,
Have not devised this slander; I'll be hanged else.
IAGO
Fie, there is no such man! It is impossible.
DESDEMONA
If any such there be, heaven pardon him.
EMILIA
A halter pardon him and hell gnaw his bones!
Why should he call her whore? Who keeps her company?
What place, what time, what form, what likelihood?
The Moor's abused by some most villainous knave,
Some base notorious knave, some scurvy fellow.
O heaven, that such companions thou'dst unfold,
And put in every honest hand a whip
To lash the rascals naked through the world,
Even from the east to th'west!
IAGO   Speak within door.
EMILIA
O fie upon them! Some such squire he was
That turned your wit the seamy side without
And made you to suspect me with the Moor.
IAGO
You are a fool, go to.
DESDEMONA   O good Iago,
What shall I do to win my lord again?
Good friend, go to him; for, by this light of heaven,
I know not low I lost him. Here I kneel:

ACT IV SCENE II

127 Beshrew: curse, damn.

128 trick: strange way.

129 I ... if: 强调 if 从句的反面意思。如 if 从句是肯定的,强调其反面的意思;反之亦然。 **eternal**: infernal.

130 busy: meddling. **insinuating**: ingratiating.

131 cogging: deceiving. **cozening**: cheating.

132 else: otherwise, if it's not so.

135 halter: hangman's noose, 绞索。

137 form: circumstance.

139 scurvy: vile, contemptible(原意为患疥癣的)。

140 that: I wish that …. **companions**: low creatures, fellows, 即下面 142 行的 rascals. **thou**: 指 heaven. **unfold**: expose.

143 Speak within door: don't shout out-of-doors lest the whole street should hear you.

144 squire: (表轻蔑的词语) fellow, rogue.

146 made you to …: 现在不定式前省略 to.

147 go to: (表示嘲弄的词语)去你的。

149 light of heaven: i. e. , the sun.

>If e'er my will did trespass'gainst his love,
>Either in discourse of thought or actual deed;
>Or that mine eyes, mine ears, or any sense
>Delighted them in any other form;
>155 Or that I do not yet, and ever did,
>And ever will — though he do shake me off
>To beggarly divorcement — love him dearly,
>Comfort forswear me! Unkindness may do much,
>And his unkindness may defeat my life,
>160 But never taint my love. I cannot say 'whore':
>It does abhor me now I speak the word;
>To do the act that might the addition earn
>Not the world's mass of vanity could make me.
>
>IAGO
>
>I pray you, be content; 'tis but his humour;
>165 The business of the state does him offence,
>And he does chide with you.
>
>DESDEMONA
>
>If'twere no other —
>
>IAGO   It is so, I warrant.
>Hark how these instruments summon to supper!
>The messengers of Venice stay the meat.
>170 Go in, and weep not; all things shall be well.
>
>*Exeunt Desdemona and Emilia*
>
>*Enter Roderigo*
>
>How now, Roderigo?
>
>RODERIGO I do not find that thou deal'st justly with me.
>
>IAGO What in the contrary?
>
>175 RODERIGO Every day thou daff'st me with some device, Iago, and rather, as it seems to me now, keep'st from me all conveniency, than suppliest me with the least advantage of hope. I will indeed no longer endure it. Nor am I yet persuaded to put up in peace what already
>180 I have foolishly suffered.

ACT IV SCENE II

152　discourse of thought: process of thinking.

153, 155　that: 接前 151 行 If, 等于 if.

154　Delighted them: delighted themselves, took delight.　**form**: i. e., man (than Othello).

156　shake me off: discard me.

157　beggarly divorcement: disgraceful divorce (separation) as a beggar.

158　Comfort: 前省略 may.　**forswear**: repudiate, forsake.

159　defeat: destroy.

161　abhor (v. t.): disgust, horrify.　**now**: 后省略 that.

162　addition: title, i. e., the name of 'whore'.

163　mass: total amount.　**vanity**: riches, showy splendour. 此两句为 Not all wordly splendour could make me do ….

164　content: calm.　**humour**: mood.

165　does him offence: worries him.

166　chide with: make a snarling sound at, find fault with.

168　Hark: listen.　**instruments**: trampets.

169　stay the meat: wait to dine.

172　justly: fairly.

175　daff'st: put off.　**device**: excuse, trick.

177　conveniency: favourable opportunity.

179　yet: still.　**put up**: tolerate.

IAGO Will you hear me, Roderigo?

RODERIGO Faith, I have heard too much; for your words and performances are no kin together.

IAGO You charge me most unjustly.

RODERIGO With naught but truth. I have wasted myself out of my means. The jewels you have had from me to deliver to Desdemona would half have corrupted a votarist. You have told me she hath received them, and returned me expectations and comforts of sudden respect and acquaintance, but I find none.

IAGO Well, go to; very well.

RODERIGO Very well, go to! I cannot go to, man, nor 'tis not very well. Nay, I think it is scurvy and begin to find myself fopped in it.

IAGO Very well.

RODERIGO I tell you, 'tis not very well. I will make myself known to Desdemona. If she will return me my jewels, I will give over my suit and repent my unlawful solicitation. If not, assure yourself I will seek satisfaction of you.

IAGO You have said now.

RODERIGO Ay, and said nothing but what I protest intendment of doing.

IAGO Why, now I see there's mettle in thee ; and even from this instant do build on thee a better opinion than ever before. Give me thy hand, Roderigo. Thou hast taken against me a most just exception; but yet I protest I have dealt most directly in thy affair.

RODERIGO It hath not appeared.

IAGO I grant indeed it hath not appeared; and your suspicion is not without wit and judgement. But, Roderigo, if thou hast that in thee indeed, which I have greater reason to believe now than ever — I mean purpose, courage, and valour — this night show it. If thou the

ACT IV SCENE II

183 **kin**: match.

184 **charge**: accuse, reproach.

185 **naught**: nothing.   **wasted**: impoverished.

186 **means**: wealth, money.

187 **corrupted**: depraved by bribery.

188 **votarist**: nun.   **them**: i. e., the jewels.

189 **comforts**: pleasures.   **sudden respect**: speedy notice.

193 **scurvy**: lousy.

194 **fopped**: cheated, fooled.

198—199 **give over**: give up.   **unlawful solicitation**: illicit courtship.

199—200 **assure yourself**: be assured.   **satisfaction**: repayment. **of**: from.

202—203 **protest**: declare.   **intendment**: intention.

204 **mettle**: fiery temper.

207 **taken ... exception**: reproached me with good reason.

208 **directly**: honestly, honourably.

211 **wit**: sense, wisdom.

next night following enjoy not Desdemona, take me from this world with treachery, and devise engines for my life.

RODERIGO Well, what is it? Is it within reason and compass?

IAGO Sir, there is especial commission come from Venice to depute Cassio in Othello's place.

RODERIGO Is that true? Why, then Othello and Desdemona return again to Venice.

IAGO O, no: he goes into Mauritania and takes away with him the fair Desdemona, unless his abode be lingered here by some accident: wherein none can be so determinate as the removing of Cassio.

RODERIGO How do you mean 'removing' of him?

IAGO Why, by making him uncapable of Othello's place — knocking out his brains.

RODERIGO And that you would have me to do?

IAGO Ay, if you dare do yourself a profit and a right. He sups tonight with a harlotry; and thither will I go to him. He knows not yet of his honourable fortune. If you will watch his going thence — which I will fashion to fall out between twelve and one — you may take him at your pleasure. I will be near to second your attempt, and he shall fall between us. Come, stand not amazed at it, but go along with me. I will show you such a necessity in his death that you shall think yourself bound to put it on him. It is now high supper-time and the night grows to waste. About it!

RODERIGO I will hear further reason for this.

IAGO And you shall be satisfied. *Exeunt*

216　engines for: plots against.

218　compass: proper bounds or limits.

219　commission: 委任书。

220　depute: appoint.

224—225　abode: stay.　　**lingered**: prolonged.　　**wherein**: in which.　**none**: nothing.

226　determinate: decisive, effective.　　**removing**: removal, i. e., killing off.

228　uncapable of: unable to take.

231　do: gain for, win for.

232　harlotry: harlot.

234　fashion: contrive, cause.

235　fall out: happen, take place.　　**take**: get, i. e., kill.

236　second(v. t.): support, help.

237　fall: die.

240　put: impose.　　**high**: overdue.

241　grows to waste: wastes away.　　**About it!**: Let's go about it! 准备干起来吧!

243　satisfied: convinced.

SCENE III

IV. iii   *Enter Othello, Lodovico, Desdemona, Emilia,*
           and attendants

LODOVICO

　I do beseech you, sir, trouble yourself no further.

OTHELLO

　O, pardon me: 'twill do me good to walk.

LODOVICO

　Madam, good night. I humbly thank you ladyship.

DESDEMONA

　Your honour is most welcome.

OTHELLO   Will you walk, sir?

5　O, Desdemona!

DESDEMONA

　My lord?

OTHELLO   Get you to bed on th'instant. I will be returned forthwith. Dismiss your attendant there. Look't be done.

DESDEMONA   I will, my lord.

　　　　　　　　Exeunt Othello, Lodovico, and attendants

EMILIA

10　How goes it now? He looks gentler than he did.

DESDEMONA

　He says he will return incontinent.

　He hath commanded me to go to bed,

　And bade me to dismiss you.

EMILIA   Dismiss me?

DESDEMONA

　It was his bidding: therefore, good Emilia,

15　Give me my nightly wearing, and adieu.

　We must not now displease him.

EMILIA

IV. iii

    4   **Your honour**: 大人，阁下。

    7—8   **on th'instant**: at once.   **be returned**: return.

    8   **forthwith**: immediately.   **Look't**: see that it.

    11   **incontinent** (adv.): soon.

    14   **bidding**: order.

    15   **nightly wearing**: nightgown.

I would you had never seen him.

DESDEMONA

So would not I: my love doth so approve him
That even his stubbornness, his checks, his frowns —
Prithee, unpin me — have grace and favour in them.

EMILIA

I have laid those sheets, you bade me, on the bed.

DESDEMONA

All's one. Good faith, how foolish are our minds!
If I do die before thee, prithee shroud me
In one of those same sheets.

EMILIA   Come, come, you talk.

DESDEMONA

My mother had a maid called Barbary:
She was in love; and he she loved proved mad
And did forsake her. She had a song of willow;
An old thing 'twas; but it expressed her fortune,
And she died singing it. That song tonight
Will not go from my mind; I have much to do
But to go hang my head all at one side,
And sing it like poor Barbary — prithee, dispatch.

EMILIA

Shall I go fetch your night-gown?

DESDEMONA   No, unpin me here.

This Lodovico is a proper man.

EMILIA

A very handsome man.

DESDEMONA   He speaks well.

EMILIA I know a lady in Venice would have walked barefoot to Palestine for a touch of his nether lip.

DESDEMONA (*sings*)

The poor soul sat sighing by a sycamore tree,
Sing all a green willow;
Her hand on her bosom, her head on her knee,

ACT IV SCENE III

17 would: wish.

18 approve: favour, command，赞许。

19 stubbornness: roughness.　**checks**: rebukes.

20 unpin: take the pins out of my hair.　**favour**: attraction, charm.

21 those sheets: i. e., the wedding sheets. 见 IV. ii 109。

22 All's one: It doesn't matter.

24 Come, come: 好啦,好啦(安慰语)。　**you talk**: i. e., talk nonsense, prattle.

26 he: the man.　**mad**: wild, i. e., faithless.

27 song of willow: song of unhappy love,英国 16 世纪一首流行的关于失恋的忧伤歌曲,见下文。

30—31 have much to do/But to go hang: can hardly avoid (refrain from) hanging.

31 at one side: aside.

32 dispatch: be quick about it.

34 proper: nice, fine.

36 would: 前省略 who.

37 Palestine: 巴勒斯坦当时许多基督徒前往朝圣,路途遥远而艰难。　**nether**: lower.

38 sycamore tree: 枫树。

　　　　Sing willow, willow, willow;
　　The fresh streams ran by her and murmured her moans;
　　　　Sing willow, willow, willow;
　　Her salt tears fell from her and softened the stones —
　　　　(*She speaks*)
45　Lay by these.
　　　　(*She sings*)
　　　　Sing willow, willow, willow —
　　　　(*She speaks*)
　　Prithee hie thee; he'll come anon.
　　　　(*She sings*)
　　Sing all a green willow must be my garland.
　　Let nobody blame him; his scorn I approve —
　　　　(*She speaks*)
50　Nay, that's not next. Hark, who is't that knocks?
　　EMILIA　It's the wind.
　　DESDEMONA　(*sings*)
　　　I called my love false love, but what said he then?
　　　　Sing willow, willow, willow;
　　　If I court moe women, you'll couch with moe men.
　　　　(*She speaks*)
55　So get thee gone; good night. Mine eyes do itch;
　　Does that bode weeping?
　　EMILIA　　　　　　　　'Tis neither here nor there.
　　DESDEMONA
　　　I have heard it said so. O, these men, these men!
　　　Dost thou in conscience think — tell me, Emilia —
　　　That there be women do abuse their husbands
　　　In such gross kind?
60　EMILIA　　　　　There be some such, no question.
　　DESDEMONA
　　　Wouldst thou do such a deed for all the world?
　　EMILIA
　　　Why, would not you?

ACT IV SCENE III

45 Lay by: put aside.　**these**: 可能指脱下的外衣。

47 hie: hurry.

49 approve: like, am pleased with.

52 love (n.): lover.

54 moe: more.　**couch**: lie, sleep.

55 eyes do itch: 犹中国人说眼皮跳。

56 bode: forebode, 预兆。　**'Tis ... there**: 不着边际, 无关(风马牛)。

58 in conscience: i. e., in all truth.

59 do: 前省略 who.　**abuse**: deceive.　**gross kind**: vicious (flagrant) way.

62 by ... light: I swear by this moonlight.

DESDEMONA   No, by this heavenly light.

EMILIA Nor I neither by this heavenly light; I might do't as well i'th'dark.

65 DESDEMONA Wouldst thou do such a deed for all the world?

EMILIA The world's a huge thing; it is a great price for a small vice.

DESDEMONA In troth, I think thou wouldst not.

70 EMILIA In troth I think I should, and undo't when I had done it. Marry, I would not do such a thing for a joint ring, nor for measures of lawn, nor for gowns, petticoats, nor caps, nor any petty exhibition. But for all the whole world! Ud's pity, who would not make her

75 husbnad a cuckold, to make him a monarch? I should venture purgatory for't.

DESDEMONA Beshrew me, if I would do such a wrong for the whole world!

EMILIA Why, the wrong is but a wrong i'th'world; and

80 having the world for your labour, 'tis a wrong in your own world, and you might quickly make it right.

DESDEMONA I do not think there is any such woman.

EMILIA Yes, a dozen; and as many to th'vantage as would store the world they played for.

85 But I do think it is their husbands' faults
If wives do fall. Say that they slack their duties,
And pour our treasures into foreign laps;
Or else break out in peevish jealousies,
Throwing restraint upon us; or say they strike us,

90 Or scant our former having in despite —
Why, we have galls, and though we have some grace,
Yet have we some revenge. Let husbands know
Their wives have sense like them; they see and smell,
And have their palates both for sweet and sour

95 As husbands have. What is it that they do,

63 Nor I neither：过去的用法，两个否定相当于一个否定。
69 troth：truth.
70 undo：annul, make amends for, 取消，想法补救。
72 joint ring：finger ring made in two halves.　**measures**：lengths of lawn, finest linen.
73 petty exhibition：small gift of money.
74 Ud's pity：God's pity.
76 venture purgatory：risk the torment of purgatory.
77 Beshrew：curse.
83 to th'vantage：to boot, more.
84 store：fill up, populate.　**played**：①gambled；②sported sexually.
86 slack：neglect.　**duties**：i. e., marital duties.
87 our treasures：i. e., semen that is due to us.
88 peevish：silly.
89 Throwing：putting, placing.
90 scant our former having：cut down our allowance (of sexual enjoyment).　**in despite**：to spite us.
91 galls：spiriting to resent injury.　**grace**：kindness, virtue.
93 sense：physical sense.

When they change us for others? Is it sport?
I think it is. And doth affection breed it?
I think it doth. Is't frailty that thus errs?
It is so too. And have not we affections,
Desires for sport, and frailty, as men have?
Then let them use us well: else let them know
The ills we do, their ills instruct us so.

DESDEMONA

Good night, good night. God me such uses send,
Not to pick bad from bad, but by bad mend! *Exeunt*

96　sport：sexual pastime.
97　affection：passion.
98　frailty：weakness in character.
101　use：①treat；②entertain sexually.
102　ills：offences.
103　uses：practice.
104　Not ... mend：Not to follow a bad example, but be warned and benefit from it.

ACT V

SCENE I

V. i   *Enter Iago and Roderigo*

IAGO

Here, stand behind this bulk; straight will he come.
Wear thy good rapier bare, and put it home.
Quick, quick; fear nothing: I'll be at thy elbow.
It makes us, or it mars us; think on that,
5   And fix most firm thy resolution.

RODERIGO

Be near at hand; I may miscarry in't.

IAGO

Here, at thy hand: be bold, and take thy stand.

He retires

RODERIGO

I have no great devotion to the deed,
And yet he hath given me satisfying reasons.
10   'Tis but a man gone. Forth my sword! He dies!

IAGO

I have rubbed this young quat almost to the sense,
And he grows angry. Now, whether he kill Cassio,
Or Cassio him, or each do kill the other,
Every way makes my gain. Live Roderigo,
15   He calls me to a restitution large
Of gold and jewels, that I bobbed from him
As gifts to Desdemona.
It must not be. If Cassio do remain
He hath a daily beauty in his life
20   That makes me ugly; and besides, the Moor

V. i

1 bulk: stall outside a shop,商店前的货摊。 **straight**: straightway, immediately.

2 bare: unsheathed. **put it home**: 向要害处刺进去。

4 It … us: It makes or spoils our fortune,成败在此一举。

7 at thy hand: (I am) near you. **take thy stand**: 摆好你的架势。

8 devotion to: enthusiasm for.

10 gone: dead.

11 young quat: little pimple,转义为 insignificant person. **rubbed … sense**: rubbed to the quick (to the raw),擦到了他最敏感的地方。

14 makes my gain: gives me profit, serves my purpose. **Live Roderigo**: Should Roderigo live.

15 calls: would call upon. **restitution**: reparation, return.

16 bobbed: cheated, swindled.

20 makes me ugly: i. e., by contrast.

May unfold me to him — there stand I in much peril.
No, he must die. But soft, I hear him coming.
  Enter Cassio

RODERIGO

I know his gait; 'tis he. Villain, thou diest!

CASSIO

That thrust had been mine enemy indeed,
25 But that my coat is better than thou think'st.
I will make proof of thine.
  He wounds Roderigo

RODERIGO   O, I am slain!
  Iago wounds Cassio in the leg, and exit

CASSIO

I am maimed for ever. Help, ho! Murder, murder!
  Enter Othello, above

OTHELLO

The voice of Cassio: Iago keeps his word.

RODERIGO

O, villain that I am!

OTHELLO   It is even so.

CASSIO

30 O, help, ho! Light! A surgeon!

OTHELLO

'Tis he! O brave Iago, honest and just,
That hast such noble sense of thy friend's wrong,
Thou teachest me! Minion, your dear lies dead,
And your unblest fate hies. Strumpet, I come!
35 Forth of my heart those charms, thine eyes, are blotted;
Thy bed, lust-stained, shall with lust's blood be spotted.   *Exit Othello*
  Enter Lodovico and Gratiano

CASSIO

What, ho! No watch? No passage? Murder, murder!

21 **unfold**: expose, reveal.
22 **soft**: stay,且慢。
24 **had been**: would have been.   **enemy**: something that is fatal or deadly.
25 **But**: if not,要不是。   **better**: tougher.
26 **make proof of**: test (in a duel).
27 **maimed**: crippled, disabled.
29 **villain that I am!**: What a villain I am!
32 **sense of**: feeling of, sympathy for.
33 **Minion**: hussy 指 Desdemona.   **dear**: lover.
34 **your ... hies**: Your cursed fate will hasten to its doom.
35 **Forth of**: from out.   **blotted**: erased,抹掉。
37 **watch**: night patrol, guard.   **passage**: passers-by.

GRATIANO

'Tis some mischance; the cry is very direful.

CASSIO

O, help!

LODOVICO

40 Hark!

RODERIGO

O wretched villain!

LODOVICO

Two or three groan. It is a heavy night.
These may be counterfeits. Let's think't unsafe
To come in to the cry without more help.

RODERIGO

45 Nobody come? Then shall I bleed to death.

LODOVICO

Hark!

Enter Iago, with a light

GRATIANO

Here's one comes in his shirt, with light and weapons.

IAGO

Who's there? Whose noise is this that cries on murder?

LODOVICO

We do not know.

IAGO   Did you not hear a cry?

CASSIO

Here, here; for heaven's sake help me!

50 IAGO   What's the matter?

GRATIANO

This is Othello's Ancient, as I take it.

LODOVICO

The same indeed, a very valiant fellow.

IAGO

What are you here, that cry so grievously?

CASSIO

38 **mischance**: misfortune, accident. **direful**: terrible.
42 **heavy**: dark.
43 **counterfeits**: fakes, shams, 冒充者。
44 **come in to**: approach.
48 **cries on**: cries out.
51 **as I take it**: I suppose.
53 **What**: who. **grievously**: miserably, sorrowfully.

Iago? O, I am spoiled, undone by villains!
Give me some help.

IAGO

O me, Lieutenant! What villains have done this?

CASSIO

I think that one of them is hereabout
And cannot make away.

IAGO   O treacherous villains!
What are you there? Come in, and give some help.

RODERIGO

O, help me here!

CASSIO

That's one of them.

IAGO   O murd'rous slave! O villain!

He stabs Roderigo

RODERIGO

O damned Iago! O inhuman dog!

He faints

IAGO

Kill men i'th'dark? Where be these bloody thieves?
How silent is this town! Ho, murder, murder!

Lodovico and Gratiano come forward

What may you be? Are you of good or evil?

LODOVICO

As you shall prove us, praise us.

IAGO

Signor Lodovico?

LODOVICO

He, sir.

IAGO

I cry you mercy. Here's Cassio hurt by villains.

GRATIANO

Cassio?

IAGO

ACT V SCENE I

54 spoiled: badly (fatally) injured. **undone:** ruined.
57 hereabout: about this place, nearby.
58 make away: escape, run away.
59, 65 What: Who.
63 Where be: where can be.
65 of good or evil: good or evil (in nature, intention, etc).
69 cry you mercy: beg your pardon.

How is't, brother?

CASSIO

My leg is cut in two.

IAGO   Marry, heaven forbid!

Light, gentlemen. I'll bind it with my shirt.

Enter Bianca

BIANCA

What is the matter, ho? Who is't that cried?

IAGO

75 Who is't that cried?

BIANCA

O, my dear Cassio, my sweet Cassio,

O Cassio, Cassio, Cassio!

IAGO

O notable strumpet! Cassio, may you suspect

Who they should be that have thus mangled you?

CASSIO

80 No.

GRATIANO

I am sorry to find you thus: I have been to seek you.

IAGO

Lend me a garter: so. O, for a chair

To bear him easily hence!

BIANCA   Alas, he faints!

O Cassio, Cassio, Cassio!

IAGO

85 Gentlemen all, I do suspect this trash

To be a party in this injury.

Patience awhile, good Cassio. Come, come,

Lend me a light. Know we this face or no?

Alas, my friend, and my dear countryman

90 Roderigo? No — yes, sure — O heaven, Roderigo!

GRATIANO

What! Of Venice?

78　notable: notorious.

79　mangled: cut into pieces.

81　to seek: looking for.

82　garter: some material to bind a wound with.　　**chair**: litter, sedan chair.

83　easily: at ease, comfortably.

85　trash: disreputable person,贱货。

86　party: participant.

IAGO

Even he, sir. Did you know him?

GRATIANO   Know him? Ay.

IAGO

Signor Gratiano? I cry your gentle pardon.
These bloody accidents must excuse my manners
95 That so neglected you.

GRATIANO   I am glad to see you.

IAGO

How do you, Cassio? O, a chair, a chair!

GRATIANO

Roderigo!

IAGO

He, he, 'tis he.

Enter attendants with chair

O, that's well said, the chair!
Some good men bear him carefully from hence.
100 I'll fetch the General's surgeon. For you, mistress,
Save you your labour. He that lies slain here, Cassio,
Was my dear friend. What malice was between you?

CASSIO

None in the world, nor do I know the man.

IAGO

(*to Bianca*) What, look you pale? O, bear him out
o'th' air.

Cassio is borne in. Roderigo's body is removed

105 Stay you, good gentlemen. Look you pale, mistress?
Do you perceive the gastness of her eye?
Nay, if you stare, we shall hear more anon.
Behold her well; I pray you look upon her.
Do you see, gentlemen? Nay, guiltiness will speak
110 Though tongues were out of use.

Enter Emilia

EMILIA

ACT V SCENE I 233

93 gentle: noble.

94 accidents: sudden events.

94—95 my manners/That so neglected: the manners of me who so neglected.

98 well said: well done.

100 For: as for.

101 Save you: you can save.

104 bear him out o'th'air: carry him indoors.

106 gastness: ghastly look.

107 anon: soon.

108 Behold: observe.

'Las, what's the matter? What's the matter, husband?
IAGO
Cassio hath here been set on in the dark
By Roderigo and fellows that are scaped:
He's almost slain and Roderigo quite.
EMILIA
Alas, good gentleman! Alas, good Cassio!
IAGO
This is the fruit of whoring. Prithee, Emilia,
Go know of Cassio where he supped tonight.
What, do you shake at that?
BIANCA
He supped at my house, but I therefore shake not.
IAGO
O, did he so? I charge you go with me.
EMILIA
O, fie upon thee, strumpet!
BIANCA
I am no strumpet, but of life as honest
As you that thus abuse me.
EMILIA   As I? Foh! Fie upon thee!
IAGO
Kind gentlemen, let's see poor Cassio dressed.
Come, mistress, you must tell's another tale.
Emilia, run you to the citadel,
And tell my lord and lady what hath happed.
Will you go on afore? (*Aside*) This is the night
That either makes me, or fordoes me quite.   *Exeunt*

SCENE II

V. ii   *Enter Othello, with a light, Desdemona in her bed*

OTHELLO
It is the cause, it is the cause, my soul:

111 **'Las**: Alas.
112 **set on**: attacked.
113 **are scaped**: have escaped.
114 **quite**: quite slain, completely dead.
117 **know of**: learn from, ask.
119 **therefore shake not**: do not shake because of that.
120 **charge**: order.
122 **honest**: chaste.
123 **Foh**: (鄙视与憎恶之词)呸。
124 **dressed**: bandaged.
127 **happed**: happened.
128 **afore**: before, in front.
129 **makes me**: makes my fortune.   **fordoes me**: ruins me.

V. ii

1 **It**: i.e., Desdemona's supposed unfaithfulness.

Let me not name it to you, you chaste stars!
It is the cause. Yet I'll not shed her blood,
Nor scar that whiter skin of hers than snow,
And smooth as monumental alabaster:
Yet she must die, else she'll betray more men.
Put out the light, and then put out the light:
If I quench thee, thou flaming minister,
I can again thy former light restore,
Should I repent me; but once put out thy light,
Thou cunning'st pattern of excelling nature,
I know not where is that Promethean heat
That can thy light relume. When I have plucked thy rose,
I cannot give it vital growth again,
It needs must wither. I'll smell it on the tree.
    He kisses her
O balmy breath, that dost almost persuade
Justice to break her sword! One more, one more.
Be thus when thou art dead and I will kill thee,
And love thee after. One more, and this the last.
So sweet was ne'er so fatal. I must weep.
But they are cruel tears; this sorrow's heavenly —
It strikes where it doth love. She wakes.

DESDEMONA

Who's there? Othello?

OTHELLO

Ay, Desdemona.

DESDEMONA   Will you come to bed, my lord?

OTHELLO

Have you prayed tonight, Desdemona?

DESDEMONA   Ay, my lord.

OTHELLO

If you bethink yourself of any crime
Unreconciled as yet to heaven and grace,

ACT V SCENE II

4 whiter：正常位置在 than 之前。

5 alabaster：a kind of gypsum，雪花石膏。

6 else：otherwise.

7 light：①the light he is carrying；②the light of Desdemona's life.

8 quench：put out. **minister**：servant.

11 cunning'st pattern：the most skilfully fashioned figure.

12 Promethean (adj.)：of Prometheus 希腊神话中的巨人（Titan），为了替人类偷天火而遭上帝的惩罚。Promethean fire 意谓 divine fire.

13 relume：rekindle.

15 needs：inevitably, absolutely，与 must 连用。

16 balmy：sweet.

17 Justice：希腊神话中的正义女神，蒙着双眼，一手执剑，一手执天平。Othello 自命为正义的执行者。

20 So sweet：前面省略 anything.

21 cruel：unrelenting, ruthless.

22 参看《圣经·新约·希伯来书》第 12 章 6 节"whom the Lord loveth he chasteneth."

26 bethink yourself of：think of, recollect. **crime**：sin.

27 Unreconciled … grace：for which you have not yet obtained heaven's forgiveness and God's grace.

Solicit for it straight.
DESDEMONA

Alack, my lord, what may you mean by that?
OTHELLO

Well, do it, and be brief; I will walk by:
I would not kill thy unprepared spirit;
No — heaven forfend! — I would not kill thy soul.
DESDEMONA

Talk you of killing?
OTHELLO   Ay, I do.
DESDEMONA   Then heaven
Have mercy on me!
OTHELLO   Amen, with all my heart!
DESDEMONA

If you say so, I hope you will not kill me.
OTHELLO

Hum!
DESDEMONA

And yet I fear you: for you're fatal then
When your eyes roll so. Why I should fear I know not,
Since guiltiness I know not; but yet I feel I fear.
OTHELLO

Think on thy sins.
DESDEMONA   They are loves I bear to you.
OTHELLO

Ay, and for that thou diest.
DESDEMONA

That death's unnatural that kills for loving.
Alas, why gnaw you so your nether lip?
Some bloody passion shakes your very frame:
These are portènts; but yet I hope, I hope
They do not point on me.
OTHELLO   Peace, and be still!
DESDEMONA

28 Solicit: petition, pray.　**it**: God's grace.　**straight**: at once.

31 基督教认为人死前未做忏悔祈祷,则死者灵魂将入地狱。**spirit**: soul.

32 forfend: forbid.

34 Amen: So be it, 阿门(基督教祈祷中的赞同语)。

37 fatal: deadly.

40 loves: 伊丽莎白时代抽象名词可加 s 成复数。

42 That ... loving: If somebody is killed because of love, that death is against the laws of nature.

45 portènts: signs fortelling disaster.

46 point on: aim at.　**Peace**: quiet, silence.　**still**: silence.

I will — so. What's the matter?
OTHELLO
That handkerchief which I so loved and gave thee,
Thou gav'st to Cassio.
DESDEMONA   No, by my life and soul!
Send for the man and ask him.
OTHELLO   Sweet soul, take heed,
Take heed of perjury; thou art on thy death-bed.
DESDEMONA
Ay, but not yet to die.
OTHELLO   Yes, presently.
Therefore confess thee freely of thy sin;
For to deny each article with oath
Cannot remove nor choke the strong conception
That I do groan withal. Thou art to die.
DESDEMONA
Then Lord have mercy on me!
OTHELLO   I say, amen.
DESDEMONA
And have you mercy too! I never did
Offend you in my life; never loved Cassio
But with such general warranty of heaven
As I might love. I never gave him token.
OTHELLO
By heaven, I saw my handkerchief in's hand!
O perjured woman! Thou dost stone my heart,
And mak'st me call what I intend to do
A murder, which I thought a sacrifice.
I saw the handkerchief.
DESDEMONA   He found it then.
I never gave it him. Send for him hither.
Let him confess a truth.
OTHELLO   He hath confessed.
DESDEMONA

47 What's the matter?：此处 Othello 伸手向 Desdemona 索物。
49 by：i. e. , I swear by.
51 perjury：false oath,伪誓是很严重的,临终时可导致灵魂下地狱。
52 Ay：ay me = alas.　　**presently**：at once.
53 freely：readily.
55 conception：purpose, plan.
56 withal：with.
59 Offend：wrong.
60 warranty：permission.
63 stone (v. t.)：turn to stone, harden.
65 sacrifice：offering,神前献祭。

What, my lord?

OTHELLO

70 That he hath used thee.

DESDEMONA How? Unlawfully?

OTHELLO

Ay.

DESDEMONA

He will not say so.

OTHELLO No, his mouth is stopped;
Honest Iago hath ta'en order for't.

DESDEMONA

O, my fear interprets! What, is he dead?

OTHELLO

75 Had all his hairs been lives, my great revenge
Had stomach for them all.

DESDEMONA

Alas, he is betrayed, and I undone.

OTHELLO

Out, strumpet! Weep'st thou for him to my face?

DESDEMONA

O banish me, my lord, but kill me not!

OTHELLO

80 Down, strumpet!

DESDEMONA

Kill me tomorrow; let me live tonight!

OTHELLO

Nay, if you strive —

DESDEMONA

But half an hour!

OTHELLO Being done, there is no pause.

DESDEMONA

But while I say one prayer!

OTHELLO It is too late.

DESDEMONA

ACT V SCENE II

70 used: made use of (for purpose of sexual pleasures).
72 stopped: closed.
73 ta'en order: taken measures.
74 interprets: finds explanation.
76 stomach: appetite, capacity.
78 Out (interj.): exclamation of abhorence, reproach of indignation.
83 Being done: since justice has begun its course.
84 But: only.

85   O Lord, Lord, Lord!
> *He smothers her*

EMILIA
> (*without*) My lord, my lord! What, ho! My lord, my lord!

OTHELLO
> What noise is this? Not dead? Not yet quite dead?
> I, that am cruel, am yet merciful:
> I would not have thee linger in thy pain.

90   So, so.

EMILIA (*without*) What, ho! My lord, my lord!

OTHELLO   Who's there?

EMILIA
> (*without*) O, good my lord, I'd speak a word with you.

OTHELLO
> Yes, 'tis Emilia. — By and by. — She's dead.
> 'Tis like she comes to speak of Cassio's death:
> The noise was high. Ha! No more moving?

95   Still as the grave. Shall she come in? Were't good?
I think she stirs again. No. What's best to do?
If she come in, she'll sure speak to my wife —
My wife! My wife! What wife? I have no wife.
O, insupportable? O heavy hour!

100   Methinks it should be now a huge eclipse
Of sun and moon, and that th'affrighted globe
Should yawn at alteration.

EMILIA   I do beseech you
> That I may speak with you. O, good my lord!

OTHELLO
> I had forgot thee. O, come in, Emilia.

105   Soft; by and by. Let me the curtains draw.
Where art thou? (*He unlocks door.*) What's the matter with thee now?

ACT V SCENE II

smothers (后舞台提示): suffocates, 闷死。

90 So: well.

92 By and by: 等一等。

93 like: likely that.

94 high: loud.

95 Still: quiet.

97 sure: surely.

99 insupportable: intolerable, insufferable. **heavy**: sad, sorrowful.

100 eclipse: 晦暗, 蚀。

101 globe: 指地球。

102 yawn: gape (as in an earthly wake). **alteration**: monstrous changes.

104 forgot: forgotten.

105 Soft: quietly, quently.

Enter Emilia

EMILIA

O, my good lord, yonder's foul murder done.

OTHELLO

What! Now?

EMILIA

But now, my lord.

OTHELLO

110 It is the very error of the moon;
She comes more nearer earth than she was wont,
And makes men mad.

EMILIA

Cassio, my lord, hath killed a young Venetian
Called Roderigo.

OTHELLO   Roderigo killed?
And Cassio killed?

115 EMILIA   No, Cassio is not killed.

OTHELLO

Not Cassio killed! Then murder's out of tune,
And sweet revenge grows harsh.

DESDEMONA

O, falsely, falsely murdered!

EMILIA   O Lord! What cry is that?

OTHELLO

That? What?

EMILIA

120 Out and alas, that was my lady's voice!
She draws back the curtains

Help, help, ho, help! O, lady, speak again!
Sweet Desdemona, O sweet mistress, speak!

DESDEMONA

A guiltless death I die.

EMILIA

O, who hath done this deed?

110 error: aberration, going astray from its course.

111 She: 月亮用阴性。　**more nearer**: 双重比较级,当时常用。中世纪相信,月亮异常会使人丧失理智。

120 Out and alas: (感叹语)哎哟, out intensifies alas.

DESDEMONA

125 Nobody — I myself — farewell.
Commend me to my kind lord — O, farewell! *She dies*

OTHELLO

Why, how should she be murdered?

EMILIA   Alas, who knows?

OTHELLO

You heard her say herself it was not I.

EMILIA

She said so: I must needs report the truth.

OTHELLO

130 She's like a liar gone to burning hell:
'Twas I that killed her.

EMILIA   O, the more angel she,
And you the blacker devil!

OTHELLO

She turned to folly; and she was a whore.

EMILIA

Thou dost belie her, and thou art a devil.

OTHELLO

135 She was false as water.

EMILIA   Thou art rash as fire to say
That she was false. O, she was heavenly true!

OTHELLO

Cassio did top her: ask thy husband else.
O, I were damned beneath all depth in hell
But that I did proceed upon just grounds
140 To this extremity. Thy husband knew it all.

EMILIA

My husband!

OTHELLO   Thy husband.

EMILIA   That she was false to wedlock?

OTHELLO

Ay, with Cassio. Nay, had she been true,

131　the more angel she：all the more is she an angel.

133　folly：wantonness.

134　belie：slander.

135　false as water：参看（英谚）unstable as water，类似汉语里的"水性杨花"。

137　top (v. t.)：mount, copulate with.　　**else**：i. e., if you don't believe me.

138　were：would be.

139　But：If ... not.

142　wedlock：matrimony, 婚姻。

>   If heaven would make me such another world
>   Of one entire and perfect chrysolite,
>   I'd not have sold her for it.

145 EMILIA   My husband!

OTHELLO
>   Ay, 'twas he that told me on her first:
>   An honest man he is, and hates the slime
>   That sticks on filthy deeds.

EMILIA   My husband!

OTHELLO
>   What needs this iterance, woman? I say thy husband.

EMILIA
150 >   O mistress, villainy hath made mocks with love!
>   My husband say that she was false?

OTHELLO   He, woman;
>   I say thy husband; dost understand the word?
>   My friend, thy husband, honest, honest Iago.

EMILIA
>   If he say so, may his pernicious soul
155 >   Rot half a grain a day! He lies to th'heart.
>   She was too fond of her most filthy bargain.

OTHELLO
>   Ha!

EMILIA
>   Do thy worst:
>   This deed of thine is no more worthy heaven
160 >   Than thou wast worthy her.

OTHELLO   Peace, you were best.

EMILIA
>   Thou hast not half that power to do me harm
>   As I have to be hurt. O gull! O dolt!
>   As ignorant as dirt! Thou hast done a deed —
>   I care not for thy sword — I'll make thee known,
165 >   Though I lost twenty lives. Help! Help, ho! Help!

143　If：even if.　**me**：for me, ethical dative.
144　chrysolite：橄榄石,金绿两色的宝石。
146　told … on：gave away secrets about.
147　slime：mire, dirt.
149　iterance：repetition.
150　made mocks with：made a mockery of.
154　pernicious：villainous, evil.
156　filthy：contemptible, disgraceful.　**bargain**：purchase, i. e., husband.
159, 160　worthy：worthy of, deserving of.
160　you were best：you had better (stop talking).
162　be hurt：endure hurt.　**gull**：dupe, fool　**dolt**：dull-witted ass.
164　care not for：don't mind.

The Moor hath killed my mistress! Murder! Murder!

Enter Montano, Gratiano, and Iago

MONTANO

What is the matter? How now, General?

EMILIA

O, are you come, Iago? You have done well,
That men must lay their murders on your neck.

GRATIANO

What is the matter?

EMILIA

Disprove this villain, if thou be'st a man:
He says thou told'st him that his wife was false.
I know thou didst not; thou'rt not such a villain.
Speak, for my heart is full.

IAGO

I told him what I thought, and told no more
Than what he found himself was apt and true.

EMILIA

But did you ever tell him she was false?

IAGO

I did.

EMILIA

You told a lie, an odious damnèd lie;
Upon my soul, a lie, a wicked lie!
She false with Cassio! Did you say with Cassio?

IAGO

With Cassio, mistress! Go to, charm your tongue.

EMILIA

I will not charm my tongue; I am bound to speak:
My mistress here lies murdered in her bed.

ALL

O heavens forfend!

EMILIA

And your reports have set the murder on.

168　well: so well.

169　lay ... on your neck: lay the blame for their murders on you (your head).

171　Disprove: prove to be false.

174　full: too fraught with emotion (to speak more).

176　apt: likely, plausible.

182　charm your tongue: be silent, hold your tongue as if a magic spell.

185　forfend: forbid.

OTHELLO
    Nay, stare not masters; it is true indeed.
GRATIANO
    'Tis a strange truth.
MONTANO
    O monstrous act!
EMILIA   Villainy, villainy, villainy!
190 I think upon't, I think — I smell't — O villainy!
    I thought so then; I'll kill myself for grief.
    O villainy, villainy!
IAGO
    What, are you mad? I charge you get you home.
EMILIA
    Good gentlemen, let me have leave to speak.
195 'Tis proper I obey him, but not now.
    Perchance, Iago, I will ne'er go home.
OTHELLO
        (*falling on bed*) O! O! O!
EMILIA   Nay, lay thee down and roar,
    For thou hast killed the sweetest innocent
    That e'er did lift up eye.
OTHELLO (*rising*)   O, she was foul!
200 I scarce did know you, uncle; there lies your niece,
    Whose breath indeed these hands have newly stopped.
    I know this act shows horrible and grim.
GRATIANO
    Poor Desdemona, I am glad thy father's dead;
    Thy match was mortal to him, and pure grief
205 Shore his old thread in twain. Did he live now,
    This sight would make him do a desperate turn,
    Yea, curse his better angel from his side,
    And fall to reprobance.
OTHELLO
    'Tis pitiful; but yet Iago knows

ACT V SCENE II

189　Villainy：wicked practice.

194　leave：permission.

196　Perchance：perhaps.

198　innocent（n.）：innocent person.

200　you, uncle：指 Gratiano,他是 Desdemona 父亲的平辈亲戚。

202　shows：appears, seems.

204　mortal：fatal.

205　Shore：shear 的过去时。罗马神话认为,人的生命为线,由命运神 the Fates 三姐妹中的一个人纺出,另一人量其长度,第三者剪断。**Did he live**：If he lived.

206　do … turn：do something desperate.

207　better angel：中世纪欧洲人认为每个人身边都隐有两个天使,一好一坏。好的天使为神所差,引人向善;坏的天使为魔鬼所差,引人向恶。　**from his side**：away.

208　fall to：fall into.　**reprobance**：damnation, i. e., by committing suicide.

209　pitiful：worthy of pity.

210	That she with Cassio hath the act of shame
	A thousand times committed. Cassio confessed it,
	And she did gratify his amorous works
	With that recognizance and pledge of love
	Which I first gave her. I saw it in his hand:
215	It was a handkerchief, an antique token
	My father gave my mother.

EMILIA   O God! O heavenly Powers!

IAGO

Zounds, hold your peace!

EMILIA   'Twill out, 'twill out. I peace?

No, I will speak as liberal as the north;
Let heaven, and men, and devils, let them all,

200   All, all cry shame against me, yet I'll speak.

IAGO

Be wise, and get you home.

EMILIA   I will not.

Iago draws his sword

GRATIANO   Fie!

Your sword upon a woman!

EMILIA

O thou dull Moor, that handkerchief thou speak'st of
I found by fortune and did give my husband,

225   For often, with a solemn earnestness —
More than indeed belonged to such a trifle —
He begged of me to steal it.

IAGO   Villainous whore!

EMILIA

She give it Cassio? No, alas, I found it
And I did give't my husband.

IAGO   Filth, thou liest!

EMILIA

230   By heaven I do not, I do not, gentlemen.
O murderous coxcomb, what should such a fool

- 210 **act of shame**: adultery.
- 212 **works**: urges, acts.
- 213 **recognizance**: token, badge, 信物。
- 217 **out**: i. e., come out into the open.
- 218 **liberal** (adv.): freely. **north**: north wind.
- 223 **dull**: stupid, obtuse.
- 224 **fortune**: good chance.
- 226 **belonged**: suited.
- 229 **Filth**: vile creature.
- 231 **coxcomb**: cock's comb, fool. 旧日弄臣头饰鸡冠似的红布。

Do with so good a wife?

OTHELLO   Are there no stones in heaven
But what serve for the thunder? Precious villain!

He runs at Iago; Montano disarms him;
Iago stabs Emilia from behind and exit

GRATIANO

The woman falls; sure he hath killed his wife.

EMILIA

235   Ay, ay; O, lay me by my mistress' side.

GRATIANO

He's gone, but his wife's killed.

MONTANO

'Tis a notorious villain. Take you this weapon,
Which I have here recovered from the Moor.
Come guard the door without; let him not pass,
240   But will him rather. I'll after that same villain,
For 'tis a damnèd slave.

Exeunt Montano and Gratiano

OTHELLO   I am not valiant neither,
But every puny whipster gets my sword.
But why should honour outlive honesty?
Let it go all.

EMILIA   What did thy song bode, lady?
245   Hark, canst thou hear me? I will play the swan
And die in music. (*Singing*) Willow, willow, willow.
Moor, she was chaste; she loved thee, cruel Moor,
So come my soul to bliss, as I speak true;
So speaking as I think, I die, I die.   *She dies*

OTHELLO

250   I have another weapon in this chamber;
It was a sword of Spain, the ice-brook's temper.
O, here it is. Uncle, I must come forth.

GRATIANO

(*within*) If thou attempt it, it will cost thee dear;

233 **But what**: except those which.　**Precious**: downright, 彻头彻尾的。

234 **sure** (adv.): surely.

238 **recovered**: taken away, retrieved, 收回。

240 **after**: 前省略 go.

241 **not … neither**: 双重否定, 等于否定。

242 **puny**: inexperienced.　**whipster**: whippersnapper. 抽鞭子发出响声的人, 转义无用而招惹人的人。

243 **honour**: 指军人的荣誉。　**honesty**: 指正直的品质。

245 **swan**: 希腊神话说, 音乐之神阿波罗的灵魂附于天鹅。传说天鹅之死其歌也善, 实际一般天鹅都不唱歌。

251 **ice-brook's temper**: wilt its steel tempered (淬炼过的) in ice-cold water.

252 **forth**: out.

Thou hast no weapon, and perforce must suffer.

OTHELLO

255 Look in upon me then, and speak with me,
Or naked as I am I will assault thee.

Enter Gratiano

GRATIANO

What is the matter?

OTHELLO   Behold, I have a weapon:
A better never did itself sustain
Upon a soldier's thigh. I have seen the day
260 That with this little arm and this good sword,
I have made my way through more impediments
Than twenty times your stop. But, O vain boast! —
Who can control his fate? — 'Tis not so now.
Be not afraid, though you do see me weaponed:
265 Here is my journey's end, here is my butt
And very sea-mark of my utmost sail.
Do you go back dismayed? 'Tis a lost fear:
Man but a rush against Othello's breast,
And he retires. Where should Othello go?

He goes to the bed

270 Now, how dost thou look now? O ill-starred wench!
Pale as thy smock! When we shall meet at compt
This look of thine will hurl my soul from heaven
And fiends will snatch at it. Cold, cold, my girl,
Even like thy chastity.
275 O cursèd, cursèd slave! Whip me, ye devils,
From the possession of this heavenly sight!
Blow me about in winds! Roast me in sulphur!
Wash me in steep-down gulfs of liquid fire!
O Desdemona! Dead Desdemona! Dead! O! O!

Enter Lodovico, Cassio in a chair, Montano and Iago with officers

LODOVICO

254　perforce：necessarily.

256　naked：unarmed.

258　itself sustain：have its place.

260　That：when.

262　stop (n.)：power to stop.

265　butt：箭靶,目的。

266　sea-mark：海上到达处的标记,如礁石或灯塔。　**sail**：sailing, trip in a ship.

267　lost：wasted, needless.

268　Man (v. t.)：aim, direct. 比较 to man a gun, 前面省略 If you. **but**：only. **rush**：灯心草。

269　retires：retreats.

270　thou：指 Desdemona. **ill-starred**：中世纪认为每个人都有天上一颗星在主宰其命运,星不好即命不好。　**wench**：girl, term of affectionate address.

271　smock：night-dress,女式宽松睡衣,长及膝盖。　**compt**：accounting,总结算。指基督教的世界末日,即最后审判日(Day of Last Judgement).

273　fiends：devils.

275　slave：Othello 自称。

276　From the possession：till I lose the sight, till I become blind.

278　steep-down gulfs：sheer whirlpools.

280   Where is this rash and most unfortunate man?
OTHELLO
　　That's he that was Othello: here I am.
LODOVICO
　　Where is that viper? Bring the villain forth.
OTHELLO
　　I look down towards his feet; but that's a fable.
　　If that thou be'st a devil, I cannot kill thee.
　　　　He wounds Iago
LODOVICO
　　Wrench his sword from him.
285 IAGO   I bleed, sir, but not killed.
OTHELLO
　　I am not sorry neither; I'd have thee live,
　　For in my sense 'tis happiness to die.
LODOVICO
　　O, thou Othello, that wast once so good,
　　Fallen in the practice of a damnèd slave,
290   What shall be said to thee?
OTHELLO   Why, anything:
　　An honourable murderer, if you will;
　　For naught did I in hate, but all in honour.
LODOVICO
　　This wretch hath part confessed his villainy.
　　Did you and he consent in Cassio's death?
OTHELLO
295   Ay.
CASSIO
　　Dear General, I never gave you cause.
OTHELLO
　　I do believe it, and I ask your pardon.
　　Will you, I pray, demand that demi-devil
　　Why he hath thus ensnared my soul and body?
IAGO

282 viper: poisonous snake (referring to Iago).

283 towards his feet: i. e. , to see if he has cloven hooves,传说魔鬼的脚如山羊蹄分趾。

289 Fallen in the practice: ①destroyed by the plotting; ②become accustomed to the way (指动不动就随便杀人)。

292 naught did I: I did nothing.   **hate** (n.): hatred.

293 part (adv.): partly.

294 consent in: agree in planning.

298 demand: ask.

300 Demand me nothing; what you know, you know:
From this time forth I never will speak word.
LODOVICO
What! Not to pray?
GRATIANO
Torments will ope your lips.
OTHELLO			Well, thou dost best.
LODOVICO
Sir, you shall understand what hath befallen,
305 Which, as I think, you know not. Here is a letter
Found in the pocket of the slain Roderigo,
And here another: the one of them imports
The death of Cassio, to be undertook
By Roderigo.
OTHELLO		O villain!
CASSIO			Most heathenish and most gross!
LODOVICO
310 Now here's another discontented paper
Found in his pocket too; and this, it seems
Roderigo meant to have sent this damnèd villain,
But that, belike, Iago, in the nick,
Came in and satisfied him.
OTHELLO			O the pernicious caitiff!
315 How came you, Cassio, by that handkerchief
That was my wife's?
CASSIO			I found it in my chamber;
And he himself confessed but even now
That there he dropped it for a special purpose
Which wrought to his desire.
OTHELLO			O fool, fool, fool!
CASSIO
320 There is besides, in Roderigo's letter,
How he upbraids Iago, that he made him
Brave me upon the watch, whereon it came

303 ope: open.
308 undertook: undertaken.
309 heathenish: unchristian.
310 discontented: full of discontent.
313 belike (adv.): probably, perhaps. **in the nick**: in the nick of time.
314 Came in: interposed. **satisfied**: paid in full, i. e., killed. **pernicious caitiff**: malicious rogue.
315 came ... by: got.
319 wrought to: worked according to.
321 upbraids: reproaches.
322 Brave (v. t.): defy. **came**: came about.

>   That I was cast; and even but now he spake
>   After long seeming dead — Iago hurt him,
> 325   Iago set him on.
>
> LODOVICO
>
>   You must forsake this room and go with us.
>   Your power and your command is taken off
>   And Cassio rules in Cyprus. For this slave,
>   If there be any cunning cruelty
> 330   That can torment him much, and hold him long,
>   It shall be his. You shall close prisoner rest,
>   Till that the nature of your fault be known
>   To the Venetian state. Come, bring him away.
>
> OTHELLO
>
>   Soft you; a word or two before you go.
> 335   I have done the state some service and they know't:
>   No more of that. I pray you in your letters
>   When you shall these unlucky deeds relate
>   Speak of me as I am: nothing extenuate,
>   Nor set down aught in malice. Then must you speak
> 340   Of one that loved not wisely, but too well;
>   Of one, not easily jealous but, being wrought,
>   Perplexed in the extreme; of one whose hand
>   Like the base Indian threw a pearl away
>   Richer than all his tribe; of one whose sùbdued eyes,
> 345   Albeit unusèd to the melting mood,
>   Drop tears as fast as the Arabian trees
>   Their med'cinable gum. Set you down this:
>   And say, besides, that in Aleppo once
>   Where a malignant and a turbaned Turk
> 350   Beat a Venetian and traduced the state,
>   I took by th'throat the circumcisèd dog
>   And smote him thus.
>   *He stabs himself*
>
> LODOVICO

323 **cast**: dismissed. **spake**: spoke.
324 **hurt**: wounded.
325 **set ... on**: instigated (him to kill Cassio).
327 **taken off**: taken away.
328 **For**: as for.
329 **cunning**: ingenious.
330 **hold him long**: keep him long alive.
331 **close prisoner rest**: remain a confined prisoner.
332 **Till that**: till. **fault**: offence.
334 **Soft you**: wait a moment.
338 **nothing extenuate**: mitigate nothing.
339 **set down**: write down. **aught**: anything.
341 **wrought**: worked on.
342 **Perplexed**: distraught.

343 **Indian**: i. e., 此字原来可能是 Judean（犹太人）。所指典故不明，但可参考《圣经·新约·马太福音》第 7 章 6 节"neither cast your pearls before the swine"。

344 **Richer**: more precious. **sùbdued eyes**: eyes overcome by grief.

345 **Albeit**: although. **melting**: softening, tearful.
346 **Arabian trees**: commiphora trees,没药树。
347 **med'cinable gum**: myrrh,没药(有药效的香树脂)。
348 **Aleppo**: 阿勒颇(今属叙利亚西北城市)。
350 **Venetian** [vi'ni:ʃən]: 威尼斯人。 **traduced**: defamed, slandered,诽谤。 **state**: 当时 Venice 为一个城邦(city state),也可指其政府。

351 **circumcisèd**: 受过割礼的。按犹太教和伊斯兰教都有这种习俗,即男子要割去包皮。参看《圣经·新约·腓立比书》第 3 章 4 节。

352 **smote**: struck.

O bloody period!

GRATIANO All that's spoke is marred!

OTHELLO

I kissed thee, ere I killed thee; no way but this,
Killing myself, to die upon a kiss.

He falls on the bed and dies

CASSIO

This did I fear, but thought he had no weapon,
For he was great of heart.

LODOVICO O, Spartan dog,
More fell than anguish, hunger, or the sea,
Look on the tragic loading of this bed:
This is thy work. The object poisons sight;
Let it be hid.

The curtains are drawn

Gratiano, keep the house
And seize upon the fortunes of the Moor,
For they succeed on you. To you, Lord Governor,
Remains the censure of this hellish villain;
The time, the place, the torture, O, enforce it!
Myself will straight aboard, and to the state
This heavy act with heavy heart relate. *Exeunt*

353 **period**: lit. full stop, end.　　**spoke**: spoken of.　　**marred**: spoiled.

357 **Spartan dog**: 以凶狠而不出声著名,这里指 Iago.

358 **fell**: cruel.

359 **loading**: burden — the dead bodies of Desdemona and Othello.

361 **keep**: guard.

362 **seize upon**: take legal possession of.

363 **succeed on**: devolve on, come down by inheritance.

364 **censure**: sentencing.

366 **straight**: go straightway.　　**state**: government.

367 **heavy**: grievous.　　**act**: event.

图书在版编目(CIP)数据

奥瑟罗 /（英）莎士比亚（Shakespeare, W.）著；申恩荣注释. —北京：商务印书馆，2014(2016.3 重印)
（莎翁戏剧经典）
ISBN 978-7-100-09897-7

Ⅰ.①奥… Ⅱ.①莎… ②申… Ⅲ.①英语—语言读物 ②剧本—英国—中世纪 Ⅳ.①H319.4:I

中国版本图书馆 CIP 数据核字(2013)第 072235 号

所有权利保留。
未经许可，不得以任何方式使用。

莎翁戏剧经典
ÀOSÈLUÓ
奥 瑟 罗
〔英〕威廉·莎士比亚 著
申恩荣 注释

商 务 印 书 馆 出 版
(北京王府井大街36号 邮政编码 100710)
商 务 印 书 馆 发 行
北 京 冠 中 印 刷 厂 印 刷
ISBN 978-7-100-09897-7

2014年8月第1版	开本 787×1092 1/32
2016年3月北京第2次印刷	印张 9¾ 插页 1

定价：30.00 元